The Ultimate Wedding
Idea Book

Also by Cynthia Muchnick

The Frugal Bride

Will You Marry Me?
The World's Most Romantic Proposals

101 Ways to Pop the Question

The Best College Admission Essays

Contents

Preface:
Will You Marry Me?

Getting engaged is a big deal. It means that you have finally made the ultimate decision to commit to one person for the rest of your life. After popping the question, many young men are surprised to discover that their girlfriends have been dreaming of this moment for as long as they can remember. So, prospective grooms, don't stress too much, but take the time to plan a proposal that is unique and appropriate to your relationship, one that will show your intended that you care enough to create a memorable proposal. You'll be surprised how many times you will be asked to tell the story of how you proposed. And if your story is truly memorable, it will become a family folk tale that you will share with others for years to come. I'm happy to share my own story to get you in the mood and perhaps inspire you, too.

My Storybook Proposal

♥   ♥   ♥   ♥   ♥

Our first kiss was at the Rodin Sculpture Garden, the most romantic spot on our college campus at Stanford University. Less than three years later, on a spring break vacation, Adam and I visited the Rodin Sculpture Garden in Paris. Having studied art history in college, I was thrilled to be with my boyfriend in this most perfect setting. After a romantic stroll through the garden, we sat down on a park bench for a friendly game of

Scrabble. (We are Scrabble buffs, and our Travel Scrabble game accompanies us everywhere!) As the game progressed, Adam managed to filch some tiles from the bag, and he placed them on the board. When he put down the word "MARRY," I giggled nervously, finding it odd that he should make such a strategically bad move and give me a chance for a triple word score.

Then he asked me, "What do you see?"

"What do I see?" I echoed.

Adam got down on one knee, pulled a ring out of the pocket of his blue jeans, and pointed to the words scattered on the board: "WILL . . . YOU . . . MARRY . . . ME"?

I was numb, shocked, excited, overwhelmed. I couldn't reply.

He repeated, "I'm asking you to be my wife. Will you?"

That was my cue. "YES! Of course I will marry you!"

What a blissful moment, frozen in my memory like a perfect photographic image. We hugged. We kissed. We called our families from a phone booth on the corner. This was the beginning of our happily ever after.

What was it about Adam's proposal that made such an impression on me and inspired me to write two books on marriage proposals and now this book? It was his care and attention to every detail of making this special moment so unforgettable. He combined the romance of Paris, the creativity of asking me with the lettered tiles of our favorite game, and the symbolism of proposing in the Parisian counterpart of the spot where we first kissed in college. The moment we decided to become teammates for life was so perfect that I had to share it with other lovers everywhere. Now, here are some tips to get *you* motivated.

Pre-Proposal Considerations

♥　　♥　　♥　　♥　　♥

Talk with your intended about marriage and the idea of getting engaged before you propose. That way you will be more certain of her response and will know each other's intentions. Communicate a lot.

•

Ask permission of her parents. It earns you brownie points and assures them that you respect their wishes.

•

If you think she will have preferences about the ring (gold versus platinum, shape of stone, setting style), be sure to ascertain them before spending a bundle. After all, your ring is going to be on her finger for the rest of her life.

•

Don't worry, you can still surprise her with an amazing proposal, even if she knows about the ring.

•

What if your proposal gets rejected? It is okay to be disappointed and even embarrassed, but consider it a blessing that you know now that you two are not meant to be, rather than having to discover it after you are engaged or even married.

•

The Ring (or Other Tokens of Engagement)

♥   ♥   ♥   ♥   ♥

Visit a local jeweler or Tiffany's to educate yourself about buying a diamond. They will teach you the four C's: color, cut, clarity, and carat.

✳

Find a reputable jeweler you can trust; in the end, that's what it all comes down to. Ask friends and family for recommendations.

✳

Do you have to spend two months' salary on a ring? That figure has become a general rule of thumb, but it is more for the benefit of jewelers than for anyone else. Spend what you are comfortable spending. Remember, you can always upgrade the ring later—at your ten-year anniversary, for instance—when funds may be more plentiful.

✳

Always have your diamond certified by the GIA (Gemological Institute of America) to ensure that it is worth the price and that you are getting what the jeweler claims he or she is selling you.

✳

Some men propose with a loose stone, then shop with their intended to choose the setting after she says yes.

✳

You can propose with an alternative item, too, if you have not looked for rings together and think she would like to help choose the setting or the shape of the stone.

✳

A brooch, family heirloom, pendant, or other keepsake makes for a nice gesture.

Location, Location, Location

♥   ♥   ♥   ♥   ♥

Think long and hard about your proposal location. If she is a private person, do not consider proposing at a baseball stadium on the huge television screen or on a live talk show where millions of viewers will witness your act. Instead, propose on a quiet beach, on a private boat, or even in your own apartment near a crackling fire. Be sure that the location suits her style.

♥

If you choose to propose at a restaurant, never give the ring to the waiter or busboy to present at dessert. He or she may run off with it and treat it as a huge tip!

♥

Also, contact the restaurant manager prior to your proposal to discuss your plan and details. They can help you if you need to have a special cake, champagne, a silver dome over her plate, or even chocolate drizzled on your dessert to spell those four magic words, "Will you marry me?"

♥

If you are taking her away somewhere special to propose, be sure to contact the hotel manager or catering director prior to your arrival so they can assist with personal touches such as candles, champagne, rose petals, bubble bath, or monogrammed bathrobes.

♥

Hotels will bend over backward to help you make your proposal memorable. Plus, they hope you'll return to their establishment for your honeymoon or future anniversaries.

♥

Warning: If you propose on or under water (while scuba diving, snorkeling, in a hot tub, in the shower, or on a boat), in the snow, or on a mountaintop, either hang on tight to the ring or have a fake one to give her. Once on dry or safe land, you can give her the real thing. Costly mishaps have been known to occur!

♥

Use Your Resources

♥   ♥   ♥   ♥   ♥

Solicit the help of friends, family, and coworkers. People love to be a part of this fun surprise.

•

Arrange for a friend or family member to secretly photograph or videotape your proposal (if you think your intended wouldn't mind). That way you can have the event recorded for posterity.

•

Questions to Consider When Planning Your Proposal

♥   ♥   ♥   ♥   ♥

What are her interests?

What activities do you enjoy doing together?

What hobbies do the two of you participate in together?

Where did you first kiss?

Where did you first meet?

Where was your first date?

What is your favorite song? Movie? Place to eat? Romantic spot or significant place where you have important talks?

What is her favorite musical group?

Do you want family or friends involved in your proposal, or would you prefer a private proposal with just the two of you?

What is your budget? Do you want an extravagant proposal or one that's not as expensive but that's extra-creative?

What talents or skills of yours could you incorporate into the proposal?

Would she consider proposing to you?

Have either of you been married before? If so, do you have children?

Have the two of you ever talked about getting married?

Have you ever looked for rings together?

Are you living together?

When is the anniversary of your first date? First kiss? Special event you shared?

What are your jobs?

Do you have a long-distance relationship?

If you are still stuck, for more great ideas and actual proposal stories to inspire and enlighten you, consult my earlier books, *Will You Marry Me? The World's Most Romantic Proposals* and *101 Ways to Pop the Question,* or e-mail me for advice at MarryMe123@aol.com.

Proposal Etiquette

♥ ♥ ♥ ♥ ♥

Be sure to practice your proposal beforehand and say the four actual words, "Will you marry me?" Otherwise, in all of your nervousness and excitement, you may blunder.

♥

If you are the forgetful type, it is okay to write a few words down on paper to reference as you declare your love.

♥

Get down on one knee when you propose. Women love this. It shows chivalry and old-fashioned charm, and she'll talk about it forever.

♥

Look into her eyes as often as you can when proposing.

♥

Proposals by Women

♥   ♥   ♥   ♥   ♥

It is the new millennium. You, too, can propose to your man. About 10 percent of the women I've interviewed have done the proposing. Most men are flattered and relieved to be let off the hook.

•

Assess the dynamics of your relationship to be sure he would not be offended by your asking.

•

Consider presenting him with a watch, bracelet, ring, or other memento to symbolize your engagement.

•

After You Get Engaged

♥   ♥   ♥   ♥   ♥

Announce your engagement in local newspapers and, more personally, to friends and family via mail, e-mail, or fax. (For more about sharing the news, see chapter 1.)

Begin to register for gifts soon after you get engaged. (For more about registering, see chapter 3.)

Some people may want to send engagement gifts, so why not have available a short list of what you two would like?

Good luck and happy proposing! Now read on with your betrothed once the deed is done.

Acknowledgments

The Ultimate Wedding Idea Book could not have been a success without the dedication, love, and support of many people:

♥ To the hundreds of brides, mothers of brides, grooms, and wedding party guests—especially Kelly Keegan, Liz Naylor, Tina Lustig, and Kim Ferguson Ruoff—and many others too numerous to list who contributed their ideas to this book, I thank you.

♥ To all of the hardworking staff at Prima Publishing—especially my acquisitions editor, Denise Sternad, who found me; my patient project editor, Michelle McCormack; my publicist, Jennifer Dougherty Hart; Brenda Ginty; and Barbara Siebert.

♥ To the Harbor View Homes Bunco Gals and my cooking class chums for their creative contributions.

♥ To my friends and fellow brides: Joanne, Nancy, Mollie, Debbie (you're next!), Marci G., Marci M., Holly, Leora, Lexi, Staci K., Teri, Nora, Chelle, Julie F., Adrienne, Janine (my unforgettable roommate!), Christie B., Nikki, Hayley, and Cheryl R.

♥ And, for real-life inspiration of Adam and Jen, Glenn and Lisa, Mike and Robin, Bobby and Tracy, and to my Florida friends and helpers Linda W. and Linda S.

♥ To those talented individuals and my esteemed colleagues who showered my work with their kind and generous words, I sincerely thank you for your praises: Diane Forden, Connie Olson Kearns (my very own extraordinary wedding coordinator!), Elizabeth Arrighi Borsting, Marcy Blum, Maria McBride-Mellinger, Beverly Clark, Michelle Merker, Brigitte Lang, and Adam Sandow.

♥ To my relatives for your love and support: Linda, Alan, Lauren, Evan; Karen, Danny, Benjamin, Sam, and David; sweet Grandma Lois; my favorite Auntie Jill and Uncle John; cousins Eric, Amy, Theo, Lucy, Gail, Andrew, Jacqueline, and Danielle; Marc, Kim, Jessica, and Blake; and Grammy Terry, my Florida promoter.

♥ To Mom and Dad Muchnick for raising such a fabulous son who has made me the luckiest bride, wife, and mother in the world. Your input and cheers always mean so much.

♥ To Mom and Dad Clumeck, the lemonade just keeps getting sweeter as I savor these passing moments. As always, thank you for your love, support, and belief in me.

♥ And finally to Adam—my groom, husband, best friend, and the most amazing father in the world to our two beautiful princes, Justin and Jacob. Thank you for always being there to cheer, support, encourage, advise, and edit. This whole adventure continues to get more exciting, and there is no one else I would rather travel down life's road with than you. Here's to many more years of happiness together as a couple and family. I love you.

— *Cynthia Clumeck Muchnick*

Introduction

And Prince Charming got down on his knee and proposed to the princess. Then the lovers rode off into the sunset on the prince's white stallion and lived happily ever after.

If you are as romantic as I am, you probably imagined that special moment way back when you were a child, long before there was a real Prince Charming in your life. However, you probably never imagined that those four magic words, "Will you marry me?," would open a Pandora's box of wedding issues. Who would have thought that your wedding and shower details, registry nightmares, budget concerns, in-law crises, bridesmaid selection dilemmas, and honeymoon destination options could become so all-consuming? You probably never realized that once you became engaged you would eat, sleep, drink, breathe, and live weddings continuously until your ultimate "I do."

As a newly engaged woman, you will be bombarded with advice by everyone from a nostalgic great-aunt at a holiday dinner to wedding professionals at bridal expos. You will be overwhelmed by the volumes of text in wedding books, bridal magazines, and wedding Web sites. Advice will pour in from coworkers, single and married friends, in-laws, children, and even your manicurist. Virtually everyone who has been a bride, groom, or wedding guest thinks he or she is an expert when it comes to planning a wedding. While others' opinions should be noted, they should also be taken with a grain of salt. Remember, this is *your* wedding.

As the voice behind *The Ultimate Wedding Idea Book*, let me state up front: I'm here for you. I've been a bride, bridesmaid (dozens of times!), sister of the bride, maid of honor, wedding coordinator, honeymooner, destination wedding guest, traditional wedding guest, and engagement expert—just to name a few of the hats I have worn. "Wedding central!" was how I answered my home telephone for several months leading up to my big day. Virtually every day, I dealt with phone calls from caterers, florists, bands, parents, in-laws, wedding party members, the rabbi, photographer, videographer, and, most important, my patient and loving fiancé. Like most brides, I was overwhelmed with details but determined to conquer the wedding beast.

Let's be real. Today's brides and grooms don't necessarily fit the traditional cookie-cutter, Martha Stewart profile. They are many different ages, with different backgrounds and visions of their ideal wedding. They may have children from previous marriages. The bride may be trying to work full-time as well as plan her wedding. The newly engaged couple might be paying for the wedding themselves and so might be looking for some cost-cutting ideas. The traditional church wedding and hall reception with all the trimmings isn't always the preferred choice of today's brides and grooms. This book was written with those contemporary needs in mind.

The Ultimate Wedding Idea Book elects to represent you: the modern-day bride. I've saved you the trouble of sifting through the hundreds of wedding publications, Web sites, and other resources available, by compiling the essential and most valuable information in one complete idea book. Thousands of couples and wedding professionals from across the nation were interviewed about their experiences and insights, and about the highlights and pitfalls they've encountered. The suggestions provided in this book were fueled by answers to such questions as "What was the best thing about your wedding, the one thing you would not change at all?"

and "What was one unique touch at your wedding that you have not seen at any other wedding?"

Why do many brides feel that they are qualified to enter the multimillion-dollar wedding industry after they have gone through planning their own wedding? Because wedding planning takes time and energy and is very emotional. We all have a vested interest in our own wedding and feel that we have become experts by going through the process. Think about it. When a couple starts to have children, why do their parents or grandparents give them so much advice? They have been through child-rearing, lived it, and have a passionate connection to it. But while every child is different and the circumstances under which each is raised are unique, so is your wedding. Remember: **It is *your* wedding**, and no one else's. Recite that mantra each day, and remind your partner that the wedding belongs to the two of you.

Weddings are expensive, and the rules have changed. Parents of the bride are not the only ones who pay for the wedding anymore. It is not uncommon for couples to pay for their own celebrations. Since the average wedding costs anywhere from $20,000 to $30,000 (and can easily cost twice that in large cities), couples are looking for alternative and more cost-effective ways to get married. This book offers a wide array of budget-minded suggestions and money-saving strategies you may have never even considered. Budgeting for your wedding doesn't mean you will have a "cheap" or "tacky" wedding, either. Rather, with some bright ideas and the benefit of testimony gleaned from couples and wedding professionals, you may be pleasantly surprised that you can save money without compromising quality.

Contemporary couples are also seeking different and creative types of weddings. Today's Generation X brides and grooms are often risk-takers who are more adventurous than those of a generation ago. Many opt for theme weddings or, at the very least, seek to incorporate modern twists on the traditional wedding. For example, "destination weddings"—weddings that take place at an exotic location—have quickly become one of the hottest wedding trends of the new millennium. Weddings at vacation destinations can eliminate family pressures, are more cost effective, are relatively easy to plan, and are often viewed as more personal and romantic by the couples themselves.

Grooms are playing a new role in wedding and honeymoon planning, too. *The Ultimate Wedding Idea Book* provides special chapters dedicated to ideas for the active, hands-on groom, the guy who wants to do more than just show up. From proposing marriage to planning the honeymoon, this book speaks to the involved groom, too. One bright idea for a groom who wants to score some extra points with his bride (as if the engagement ring purchase wasn't enough!) is to sign you both up for some dance lessons. You'll be amazed how several hours with a dance instructor can turn a bride or groom with two left feet into an almost legitimate Ginger Rogers or Fred Astaire. And you'll definitely impress your wedding guests and future in-laws with your seemingly effortless waltz, samba, salsa, or fox-trot to your wedding song.

With more than half of today's marriages ending in divorce, many weddings involve a bride or groom who has been married before. This poses many new questions in wedding planning. How can children from previous marriages be incorporated into the wedding? Can the bride wear white? Who should give the bride away? Who pays for the wedding? How do couples handle re-registering? Should the children be invited on the honeymoon (familymoon)? *The Ultimate Wedding Idea Book* will address these issues and give you suggestions and advice on how to handle sensitive and unique situations. As a special bonus, this book also offers advice and planning tips to friends and family who are throwing showers and bachelor or bachelorette parties. Further tips are offered to wedding participants who plan to make toasts to the bride and groom at the rehearsal dinner or wedding.

The Ultimate Wedding Idea Book will help eliminate your need to navigate through the deluge of wedding advice that will come your way. It serves as the perfect companion to any wedding planner that you choose to use. This book is meant to bring the culmination of research and personal experience on ideas, tips, strategies, and creative solutions to your modern-day wedding needs. *The Ultimate Wedding Idea Book* offers choices and provides ideas for special touches you may not have contemplated. You may want to read it with a highlighter, to sort through the suggestions that work for your needs and underscore what you may want to adapt and build upon. This book is not designed to be your nuts-and-bolts wedding planner, nor will it tell you everything you need to do to have a successful wedding. *The Ultimate Wedding Idea Book* is a resource full of ideas and inspiration, meant to offer you tips you may not have considered and alternatives to the traditional wedding. It aspires to increase your chances for having a wedding that fulfills *your* vision.

Here's hoping the ideas contained within these pages inspire, entertain, and enlighten you. Wishing you a happily ever after!

—*Cynthia C. Muchnick*

1

Announcing the News and Selecting Your Wedding Party

Ring the bells! Shout the joyful news from the highest mountaintop! Tell the world—you are engaged! Now it is time to spread the news and choose those who are the closest to you to be members of your wedding party.

Choosing your wedding party can be stressful, overwhelming, and even political. Should your future sister-in-law be a bridesmaid? Can a close male friend be in your wedding party? Do you have to include people in your wedding party who have included you in theirs, even if you are not very close to them anymore?

Think of selecting the members of your wedding party the way you would choose players for an all-star team. These are the people who mean the most to you and who can help you get through this exciting time

with as few complications and stresses as possible.
Here are some ideas for you.

Sharing Your News

♥   ♥   ♥   ♥   ♥

Telling Family and Friends

Some couples choose to print their own announcements to mail to family and friends. This is fine, but be
sure to still call those closest to you, tell them the news
in person, or send those outside your immediate family
and circle of friends an e-mail or a fax. Choose the
method that you are comfortable with. There are no
hard-and-fast rules.

●

Be sure to personally contact all family members and
close friends who would be offended to hear about your
news from the paper or through mutual friends. No
one wants to be the last to know.

●

Divide up your list, and have your fiancé contact his
friends and those on his side of the family.

●

Ask your parents to contact their close friends to
save you time. Just be sure that the people they contact
are among those you plan to have on your guest list.

●

Telling the World

Contact local papers, church-affiliated bulletins, college alumni magazines or newsletters, and even your fraternity/sorority organization magazine to share your happy news. Often they publish weekly or monthly announcements of engagements and weddings.

Some magazines or papers will print only wedding announcements, not engagement news. Keep a list of these so you can send them a wedding photo and news after the fact.

Check to see if your newspaper will print a picture of you and your fiancé. This will be a super souvenir for your scrapbook.

Telling Coworkers and Your Boss

Tell your boss and coworkers as soon as you are engaged so they can prepare, well in advance of your wedding date, for any emotional or work-related issues that may arise.

♥

Request wedding and honeymoon time off as soon as you choose your date.

♥

Don't let your boss catch you surfing wedding-related Web sites during your workday. This might cause concern about the impact of your wedding planning or the quality of your work.

♥

Your Wedding Party

♥   ♥   ♥   ♥   ♥

Selecting Your Party

Ask each person to be in your wedding party in a special way. Try to ask in person or, if geography limits you, call or hand-write a card or letter. When you ask, be sure to tell the person your reasons for asking—the important role he or she has played in your life—to convey what a true honor it is for you to have included them as an attendant.

●

Other honors you can bestow on friends who are not selected to be in your wedding party include having them do readings during or after your ceremony, be in charge of the wedding guest sign-in book, hand out programs at the wedding, sign your ketubah (Jewish marriage contract), or be extra ushers who escort guests to their seats.

●

When choosing your wedding attendants, think about who you would like to see in your wedding album twenty years from now.

●

Pre-Wedding Mailing

Well in advance of your wedding date, send out a mailing to members of your wedding party detailing their duties and what they can prepare before the wedding.

Make the mailing fun and upbeat. For example, prepare a "Top 10 Things to Do Before Sara and Joe's Wedding" list, itemizing such things as where and how to go about tux or bridesmaid dress fittings, any necessary travel-related information to assist those coming from far away, your e-mail address and other contact information, and important dates of pre-wedding events, including showers, bachelor/bachelorette parties, rehearsal dinners, and other gatherings.

Set up a wedding Web site where you can post information, such as where you're registered, fun photos of you and your fiancé, important dates, hotel information, locations of events, and more. You can keep updating the site as you have more information. Just remember that not all of your guests will have Internet access, so be sure that they get postal mailings containing all pertinent information.

Family and Personal Wedding Party Issues

If you have two sisters, think about making them your co-maids of honor so you don't have to show a preference. Even if you are significantly closer to one than the other, remember that getting married is a huge milestone in your life, and it is important for family to be a significant part of it.

♥

If one of your sisters is married, she could be your matron of honor and your other sister could be your maid of honor.

♥

Even if someone included you in their wedding party, there is no rule that you must include them in yours. You are not required to use your wedding as the occasion for returning a favor to someone—unless you truly feel that he or she is extremely important or close to you.

♥

To get some perspective on how many people to have in your wedding party or just on whom to ask, consult with your parents or any of their friends who were married a generation ago. Ask them how many people from their wedding party they still keep in touch with, and you may realize that your party is too big.

♥

Delegating Duties

Wedding party attendants tend to behave differently before and at your wedding depending on whether they are themselves married or single. You may be able to rely more heavily on attendants who have the benefit of personal experience with weddings. Married attendants may have an edge on the singles and often can more easily anticipate your needs and emotional issues since they have been in your situation before.

•

Consider the attendants' marital status when assigning duties. Don't assume they can understand all of your concerns. In other words, know your participants.

•

Delegate to your wedding party whatever duties you can, such as assistance in addressing and stamping invitations, tying ribbons around party favors, being your driver the day of the wedding, or assisting you in errands in the days leading up to your wedding.

•

Brides, take the best man aside sometime before the wedding, or call him in advance, to be sure he understands the schedule of the day and will herd together the male members of the wedding party in time to walk down the aisle.

•

Be certain that your best man has the rings in a safe place that will be easily accessible during the ceremony, such as a coat or pants pocket. You may want the groom to hold onto them until just before the ceremony, though, for safekeeping.

•

Have the best man be responsible for getting nutritional food and nonalcoholic beverages into the groom (and the rest of the wedding party, for that matter!) throughout the wedding day or evening. Grooms often will not openly admit their nervousness or hunger, and they have been known to faint during the ceremony.

●

Dressing the Party

You know the old adage that a woman will only wear a bridesmaid dress once? That doesn't have to be the case. Rather than trying to choose a single dress that will flatter all of your attendants, consider choosing a specific fabric or color scheme and sending samples of it to your wedding party, so each attendant can buy or make a dress that suits her body type and style.

If you have specific preferences—dress length, on or off the shoulder, strapless or not—be sure to specify them to your attendants, so there will be enough uniformity among the party.

Your maid of honor could be distinguished from the rest of the group by wearing a dress of a slightly lighter or darker shade or a different length, or by wearing a shawl or carrying a different bouquet.

For groomsmen, slacks and a sport jacket or suits are alternatives to the traditional tuxedo. The groom then could give a tie as his groomsmen gift and coordinate the tie with the bridesmaids' dresses or floral color scheme.

Attendants' Gifts

Some great gift ideas for the bridal party include en-graved picture frames, personalized stationery, mono-grammed travel kits, silver monogrammed key chains with your wedding date on them, perfume, spa gift cer-tificates, or earrings or other jewelry that you want the bridesmaids to wear for the ceremony.

♥

A new trend is to give wedding party gifts that grow, such as perennial flowers that will bloom each year to remind attendants of your special day.

♥

Groomsmen always like the typical engraved flasks, key chains, or business card holders, but how about giv-ing monogrammed golf balls, putters, or Swiss Army knives as an alternative? Tickets to a sports event that the groom and his groomsmen can attend as a group over the wedding weekend may be a fun, unique gift idea.

♥

Think about presenting gifts to your wedding party as a group—with the groomsmen and the bridesmaids together—perhaps at the wedding ceremony rehearsal or just before the rehearsal dinner. That way the mem-bers of the wedding party can be introduced to each other and learn a bit more about how each person is connected to you and your fiancé.

♥

One bride and groom decided to give individual per-sonalized gifts to each of their attendants depending on their interests. The wedding party was flattered that the

bride- and groom-to-be put so much thought into selecting each gift.

♥

Modern Wedding
Etiquette Issues

It is okay to have a different number of bridesmaids
and groomsmen. In the procession, you can pair up
men and women or single out your maid of honor
while doubling up the other bridesmaids. Feel free to
be creative.

●

If you are particularly close to a male friend and your
groom does not include him as one of his groomsmen,
rest assured that it's okay for women today to have
members of the opposite sex as their attendants. Talk
your plans over with your fiancé to be sure he is comfortable with this option. Also ask him whether he has a
female friend whom he would like to be in the party.

●

If you have a younger cousin or niece who is too old
to be a flower girl but too young to be a bridesmaid,
consider bestowing on her the honor of being a junior
bridesmaid. She can walk in the procession in a dress
that has the same color scheme as the apparel of the
wedding party.

●

Believe it or not, one bride had her dog be the ring bearer. She dressed him in a little tuxedo and tied the pillow to his back. A friend walked the dog down the aisle.

●

Final Pre-Wedding Activities

Your groom should plan a guys' day of golf, touch football, sports bar outing, or some other activity to do together with his groomsmen before the wedding, so they can have a chance to bond and hang out apart from the actual ceremony.

The Day of the Wedding

Have a "girls' day" the day of the wedding (or the day before if you have an early morning wedding), during which you do things like getting your hair and makeup done together and indulging in other types of pampering such as massages, manicures, and pedicures.

♥

Get dressed together as a wedding party. It is fun to prepare for your big day with your closest girlfriends there to share it.

♥

Assign a bridesmaid to carry your lipstick and to be in charge of other essential items for you on the day of the wedding.

♥

Prepare a wedding day Bride's Survival Kit for yourself that includes items such as lipstick, bobby pins, hair spray, a compact mirror, a comb or brush, stockings, clear nail polish for pantyhose runs, a travel sewing kit for emergency repairs, a piece of white chalk or white medical tape for any accidents that may happen to your wedding dress (makeup smudges, food spillage, loose fabric that needs to be held down, and so on), deodorant, extra copies of any passages or speeches that people will be reading at the wedding, eye drops, aspirin, bandages, a nail file, breath mints, tampons, tissues, and any other essentials that you may need.

♥

You may want to stash the kit under the sink in the bathroom you will be using or with your maid of honor's items so she can be in charge of it.

♥

Prenuptial Parties

Ahhh, the parties—and there will be many: one or more showers, the bachelor and bachelorette parties, the wedding rehearsal, and the rehearsal dinner, to name a few. But don't worry: You and your fiancé are the stars of the show, and these festive events revolve around you. Just keep your sense of humor and your wits about you, celebrate your love for each other, and enjoy the fun!

Bridesmaids and groomsmen, close friends of the bride and groom, or relatives of the couple's parents typically give a wedding shower or two for the bride, or couple's showers for both, and usually organize the bachelorette party and the bachelor party, respectively. As soon as you know who will be giving these parties for you, share this chapter with them to give them ideas.

You'll likely be intimately involved in planning the wedding rehearsal, rehearsal dinner, and actual wedding on the other hand, unless you've hired a wedding consultant.

Rehearsing for the big day and seeing the wedding party and out-of-town guests all together at the rehearsal dinner will be your final reminders that your wedding day is almost here.

Showers

♥   ♥   ♥   ♥   ♥

Theme Ideas

Send three recipe cards (or index cards) to each guest with their shower invitation. Ask them to write down their favorite appetizer, entree, and dessert recipe and to put their names and phone numbers on the recipe cards. At the shower, collect the cards and arrange them in a pretty recipe box to present to the bride. This will begin or enhance her cooking repertoire and give her a helpful contact to consult if she has trouble with a recipe.

●

Have each invitee bring a different kind of recipe: a recipe for a happy marriage. Guests can offer quotes, suggestions, and anecdotes to share with the bride to prepare her for a successful married life.

●

One hostess mailed each guest a blank photo album page with instructions to decorate it with photos, quotes, anecdotes, or other meaningful ideas for the bride-to-be. Each invitee presented her page at the shower and added it to the album for the bride-to-be to take home.

•

Fun bridal shower themes include "Around the Clock," for which each guest is preassigned a time of day to correspond to her gift, "Lingerie," "Kitchen," "Recipes," or "Holidays."

•

Couples' showers, rather than the traditional "girls-only" events, are becoming increasingly popular. Typically, evenings are better for these events.

•

For a couples' shower, be sure to choose a theme that both genders can appreciate, such as "Around the House," where each guest brings a gift that corresponds to a preassigned room of the house, or "Outdoor Activities," for which guests bring items the couple would enjoy outdoors, such as sporting equipment, beach towels, or exercise gear. The "Handy Couple" shower is a popular way for the honorees to stock up on tools and home accessories, and "That's Entertainment" is a fun theme for stereo or video equipment, CDs and videos, and maybe even a popcorn popper.

•

Smart Shower Tips

Instead of a shower guest book that people sign, try something more creative such as a wooden plate for guests to autograph with paint pens, or a champagne bottle that can be signed with metallic pens.

Mount a funny photo of the bride on a piece of matting or poster board, and have each guest write a message to her on the border. These will be fun keepsakes for her to hang or display in her future home.

If the bride's coworkers want to give her a surprise shower, they could have her boss call her into a conference room where boxed lunches and gifts await.

Shower Games, Prizes, and Favors

Door prizes are a good incentive to get people into the swing of things and break the ice.

♥

Have fun games or activities planned for the shower. Guests can bring anecdotes about the bride, compete to dress her in a toilet paper gown, or get quizzed on trivia about her and the groom.

♥

Cute shower party favors include small plants, sachets, scented soaps, candles or bath oils, a decorated tin full of colored jelly beans or pastel candies, tiny glass vases with fresh-cut flowers, homemade brownies or pretty cookies wrapped in colorful cellophane and ribbon, a box of festive tea bags or coffees, miniature books, picture frames, stationery, or pretty notepads.

♥

Bashes on a Budget

Have the event at the home of the shower hosts. There could be a potluck dinner or one cooked by the hosts and the bridesmaids.

●

Consider using potted plants, confetti, or balloons as centerpieces instead of elaborate flower bouquets.

●

Thank-Yous

At the shower, make sure the bride assigns a bridesmaid to keep a list of the gifts received and who gave them, so she won't forget anyone when she is writing her thank you notes.

A note to the bride: Of course you will write a thank you note, but don't forget to bring a gift for the hosts of your shower to show your gratitude. Flowers, wine, a fruit basket, cookie bouquet, or personalized stationery are some ideas.

Bachelor and Bachelorette Parties

♥   ♥   ♥   ♥   ♥

Planning

Bars and striptease clubs are becoming outdated as couples of the new millennium become more progressive and less sexist. Consider these ideas instead: a spa or golf club weekend getaway; a wine-tasting locale; a live sporting event or sports bar; a weekend at a beach house or ski lodge; a Las Vegas trip; a retro disco-dancing club; a karaoke bar; a Western theme bar with an electric bull and line dancing; a funky new restaurant or comedy club (be sure to let the staff know who the bachelor or bachelorette is, so he or she can be razzed!); or a ceramics-painting studio where partygoers can drink wine and decorate items for the couple's new home.

♥

Microbreweries can be rented out for groups to brew and bottle their own beer. Some establishments even have personalized label-making capabilities, so the bride and groom's names and wedding date can be printed on the bottles.

♥

Coed bachelor and bachelorette parties are also becoming a trend. Everyone's friends can celebrate together by playing a coed softball game or a round robin volleyball tournament, renting a boat and hanging out on the water, having a beach barbecue, joining in a men versus women scavenger hunt, or enjoying another fun gathering.

♥

If possible, plan the parties in advance of the wedding weekend—preferably several weeks or months in advance. That way no one suffers hangovers, exhaustion, or hard feelings on the weekend of the actual wedding.

♥

Be sure to hire a limousine or van, or at least assign a responsible designated driver, to chauffeur the party-goers. It is usually better to hire a driver than to rely on a friend, since finding parking as you move from place to place can be time consuming and will prevent that person from sharing completely in the fun.

♥

Activities

Dress the bride or groom in a way that distinguishes her or him from the bunch. Something as simple as a headband with white fabric attached to represent a wedding veil for the bride, or a "groom" sign hung around the neck of the groom, will make her or him feel embarrassed and the center of attention. (Even a baseball cap emblazoned with "bride" or "groom" will do!)

•

A scavenger hunt is a great activity. Have the bride or groom pose for pictures with members of the opposite sex that you encounter throughout the evening. The bride or groom can be required to collect naughty things from these folks such as an article of clothing, a kiss on the cheek, or an autograph.

●

Erotic magazines and videos and funny sex toys are much less expensive than hiring a stripper, and they're also less potentially harmful to the bride or groom or a raucous group of revelers. These lower-budget but still X-rated alternatives will do the trick.

●

Bring an instant camera with you on your night out to record the highlights of your evening. Later on, write captions on the pictures to chronicle the activities, and put them in a small album for the bride or groom as a memento.

●

A disposable camera will also do; just be sure to take it to a one-hour photo processing service so you'll get your pictures back quickly.

●

Girls Only!

Consider giving the bride funny gag gifts or romantic items to bring on her honeymoon, such as scented candles, sexy lingerie, a book about sex (with illustrations!), flavored body and massage oils, exotic bubble bath, or silly sex toys.

Dress the bride in a candy necklace from a gumball machine and, throughout the evening, have men you encounter bite off one candy at a time. Photograph these moments.

Order a cake shaped like male genitalia to eat at the party. It makes for great photo opportunities and funny memories.

A Final Thought for the Couple

A guys' or girls' night out is a fun way to get ready for the big day. Just don't let the male or female bonding get too out of control, or you're liable to create some premarital turmoil. Talk as a couple before you venture your separate ways for your bachelor and bachelorette parties, so you can reach some understanding about what the other is doing. That way there will be no hard feelings or shocking hangovers the day after, since you will have already discussed your concerns or expectations.

♥

Wedding Rehearsal

For the wedding rehearsal (which will probably be earlier on the day of the rehearsal dinner), have baseball caps or T-shirts printed with "bride" and "groom" for you and your fiancé to wear. You may even want to make versions for other wedding party members, such as your bridesmaids or the mother of the groom.

•

Take it one step further and have your wedding date and the bride and groom's names printed on them as well. They'll make for cute photos and keepsakes.

•

Don't forget to bring your mock bouquet as a prop to carry down the aisle; have one of your bridesmaids make it using the ribbons from your wedding shower gifts.

•

Have snacks and beverages available for members of the wedding party. Light finger foods, clear carbonated sodas, and fresh fruit are good sugar boosts on hot days. The rehearsal can be exhausting, and snacks can keep everyone on their toes and energized. Also have these foods available on the wedding day.

•

If you have hired a wedding consultant, you should generally defer to him or her at the rehearsal, but speak up if there is something you are unclear about or don't like.

•

Your wedding consultant has attended and coordinated many more weddings than you'll ever experience, so let him or her take charge and save you from having to boss around the wedding party. In other words, let him or her be the bad guy (if one is necessary).

•

Rehearsal Dinner

♥   ♥   ♥   ♥   ♥

Themes and Locations

Plan a theme for the rehearsal dinner and weave it throughout your centerpieces, attire, or entertainment. One couple had all the guests arrive in Western garb for their hoedown barbecue rehearsal dinner, complete with hay bales and square dancing, while another served up make-your-own-fajitas at a Mexican fiesta.

Consider alternative locations and styles for the rehearsal dinner, such as a private room at a fun pizza restaurant, a beach cookout, or dinner and dancing aboard a privately chartered boat.

If your in-laws are giving the rehearsal dinner and it seems as though it is getting a bit too extravagant, have your fiancé talk to his parents and pull in the reins. You want to be sure that this event does not in some way outshine the wedding day.

Enjoy the rehearsal dinner, as it will be more intimate than the wedding day and will allow you and your betrothed to mingle more substantially than on the big day.

Toasts

Encourage guests to make toasts or to bring advice for the bride and groom. You may want to include a formal request for toasts—perhaps on a particular theme, such as "advice to the bride and groom on a successful marriage"—in the rehearsal dinner invitation.

♥

If you do not plan to make a toast at your wedding, the rehearsal dinner would be a great time to give one. This more intimate group of friends and family may be a less overwhelming audience than the wedding crowd, so you may feel a bit less nervous.

♥

Be sure someone videotapes all of the toasts so you can have them memorialized forever.

♥

Put together a slide show or video presentation (or encourage your parents to do so) that includes images of the two of you growing up independently, leading up to your meeting and falling in love. Include poems, songs, or anecdotes to share with friends and family. (You can also present a slide show on the day of the wedding—during wedding party photos or while you are in the receiving line and the guests are passing the time until the meal.)

♥

Rehearsal Activities

Many of the following ideas can apply to both the rehearsal dinner and the wedding reception.

•

Have baby pictures of the two of you or fun photos of you as a couple enlarged to poster size and hung at the rehearsal area for guests to view.

•

For an even more personal touch, one bride made several posters with photos or a collage of herself and her fiancé with their friends and relatives. She put small captions beneath the photos so the guests could find themselves and see what kinds of fun experiences the bride and groom had shared with others. All of the guests really enjoyed being showcased!

•

Have a photo album or scrapbook of your relationship available for guests to peruse. (Be sure to put a member of your wedding party in charge of the album so it is not lost during the evening.)

•

One couple made a poster-board timeline of their lives and relationship with short descriptions of significant dates and events such as when and where they were born, where they went to college, how they met, where they shared their first kiss, and how he proposed. Photographs also adorned the board, which served as fun reading for guests during the rehearsal dinner and reception.

•

Talk in advance with your fiancé about who will be there from his side of the family whom you have not met before, and give him the same information for your family. Try to learn a factoid about each person so that when you meet for the first time, he or she will feel special. First impressions are key!

●

Be sure to personally welcome all of the out-of-town guests. It means so much to those who have traveled to great lengths and expense to share in your celebration.

●

Don't forget about the most important guests of all: each other. It is easy to get caught up in separate conversations with friends and family, but you two are truly the focus of the evening, so be sure your body language and love for each other are displayed for all to see.

●

3 ♥

Registering 101

Registering can be either the most fun process you and your fiancé go through together before the wedding, or the most stressful. Choosing items for your new life is an exciting way to start to visualize your future together, but it can also often bring up serious differences in personal taste and style. Once again, keep your sense of humor and enjoy the process. Remember, almost anything can be returned.

Gift Registration

♥   ♥   ♥   ♥   ♥

Why Register?

Some couples feel awkward or strange about selecting gifts for people to buy for them. If this is the case with you, it may help to think of registering as a service you are providing for family and friends as well as for yourselves.

•

As a couple, you know the most about what you would like and need, and registering allows guests to choose an item from your list that fits their price range and is the particular type of gift they want to give.

•

Registering will save you a huge amount of time by limiting your need to return or exchange items that do not appeal to you or that you already have.

•

Think of registering as a shopping spree without a cash register at the end!

•

Choosing Your Stores

In choosing where to register, check the store's customer service, return and exchange policies, and accessibility for your guests who live in other parts of the country or world. Some stores, for example, offer only store credit for gifts you return, while others give cash refunds, which may be preferable to you. Other stores have a time limit for returns.

Be aware that some department stores insist on gift receipts for returns, while others will offer you only the most recent sale price in the last thirty days for a returned gift. This can be problematic, so be sure to ask the stores about these issues prior to establishing your registry.

Many stores also have computerized gift registries (different from online registries) that allow guests to print out your registry by entering your or your groom's name into a computer.

In-store electronic gift registries as well as sales people will also assist you after your showers and wedding in keeping track of gifts that you may have received.

Be sure to check with the stores periodically to make sure that they are updating your registry as your guests purchase items.

If you want to register somewhere that does not have a gift registry program (such as a small boutique or non–chain store), consult with the store manager to see if you can leave with them a list of items you would like. Who knows? You may inspire them to create a registry!

Be aware, though, that smaller stores may have more restrictions on returns, exchanges, or back-ordered items, since they may not have access to the same quantity of items as do larger stores. They may also have higher prices. Inquire about these and other policies before committing.

✳

It is a *major faux pas* to include with your wedding invitation a list of the stores where you are registered! Invitees will ask you, friends, or family where you are registered if they choose to purchase gifts in this way.

✳

On the other hand, including the names of stores where you are registered on a shower invitation is acceptable and not inappropriate.

✳

New Trends

Some couples are turning to online bridal registries because they allow invitees immediate access to your lists from all over the country. You should still plan on registering with at least one major department store or mail-order company to provide options for guests without computer access and for those who want to actually see and touch the items that they plan to purchase.

♥

Some couples go beyond traditional gifts like china, crystal, silver, appliances, and cookware toward more practical, homeowner-oriented items such as furniture, barbecue grills, televisions, sporting goods, camping equipment, artwork, and even computers.

♥

Many couples today register at travel agencies or mortgage lenders to allow invitees to contribute toward their honeymoon or home down payment. If you choose this type of registry, though, be sure that you also have a separate registry for more traditional wedding items so guests have a gift option other than a cash contribution.

♥

Brides and grooms may also choose to be philanthropic and request that those invited make a donation to a specific charity in lieu of a gift. This is more common in second or third marriages, in which the couple are already established and do not need many items for their home.

♥

Registering for Gifts

Choosing some items may be better left up to you, the bride—such as having the final say about the china pattern—but let your groom choose things like the juicer, bread maker, or barware if he is so inclined.

●

Don't let registering together become a burden on you or the source of arguments between you and your fiancé. Granted, you two will have different tastes, but keep your sense of humor and enjoy the process.

●

Approach the process of registering with common sense. Do you really need an ice cream maker, fondue pot, or bread maker that you may use only a few times, as opposed to more practical (but less exciting) items that you will use every day, such as measuring cups and glassware?

•

Be sure to select gifts in a wide variety of price ranges.

•

One couple registered for several sets of candlesticks because they were available at a price they knew would be affordable to their guests. Then, after the wedding, they returned all but one set and used the store credit they received to complete other sets of items on their registry.

•

More expensive gifts are ideal for a group of family members, friends, or coworkers to chip in on together.

•

If you don't have a great set, register for luggage. You'll enjoy it on your honeymoon, future travels, and business trips.

•

Use in-store registry checklists to assist you in considering all that you need. Be cautious, though; since stores want you to register for a lot of items, their checklists may include some extraneous items that you don't really need.

•

China

Register for china. Even if you two don't think you'll be entertaining formally for many years, this is the time to acquire your china. After all, do you think you'll go out and buy china for each other on your tenth anniversary?

The same goes for crystal and sterling silver flatware. However, keep in mind that if you don't think many of your invitees will be able to afford these higher-priced items, you may want to use store credit later toward completing these sets.

Many everyday stemware and flatware items can be mixed in with your formal china.

Remember that you will be eating off your everyday china for a long time. What you like now may be too funky for your tastes later. Consider long-term use and preferences before choosing a pattern.

Registering for a set of all-white dishes can be a great way to get the best of both worlds. You can mix in any fun bowls, salad plates, place mats, and tablecloths more easily, and the white dishes will never go out of style.

An all-white set is also great if you like to travel and collect pottery or tableware from different regions. Virtually everything will mix in well with a set of white, so you'll get lots of flexibility and versatility from this choice.

You can choose a very simple fine china, such as a white with a single gold or blue band around the edge. This also allows you to mix in many other patterns of dishes and table accents.

Other Tips

If a gift arrives without a card, contact the store immediately. Most stores keep information on purchasers for this very reason (and for returns).

♥

Set up a wedding account for yourselves where you can deposit the checks of congratulations that may arrive after you announce your engagement.

♥

Many guests may bring checks in cards when they come to your wedding. Be sure to have your maid of honor or best man keep these for you during the event. Some couples even have a small fabric bag or box to collect cards with checks enclosed.

♥

Keep a master list of all gifts received, from what store they came, who gave them to you, and the date you wrote your thank you note so that you can have a personal record. For more on thank you notes, see chapter 20.

♥

Finally, if the wedding is canceled, you should return all gifts received.

♥

4

Wedding Invitations

Classic wedding invitations are engraved, very formal, and printed in a fancy cursive font that resembles calligraphy. As you will see below, there are fewer rules for invitations today, and they can be much less formal.

Invitations

♥   ♥   ♥   ♥   ♥

Creative Ideas

Invitations can be printed on scrolls or hand-painted on cards.

•

Some couples opt for pretty handmade papers such as those containing pressed or dried flowers.

•

You can make your own invitations, but be sure to factor in the cost of your time and what it is worth to you. More potential headaches and unforeseen costs can be associated with making your own than with the more conservative store-bought route. Be sure you are prepared for the extra work and time commitment involved.

•

Some couples design homemade invitations with photos of themselves scanned in or printed on the invitations.

•

One bride chose to literally make her own paper. She used construction paper, a blender, water, and flower petals. (Consult a craft store or a book on papermaking for more details!) Then she used tracing paper as the overlay with the invitation printed on it, and attached the pages together with ribbon. The invitations were a fraction of the cost of store-bought ones and had her handmade personal touch on each.

•

Wording

The wording of invitations has become less formal due to many factors, including the increasing number of weddings involving blended families, the greater frequency of weddings paid for mostly or entirely by the bride and groom, and the high divorce rate. Consult stationery stores, the Internet, and etiquette or wedding books to get ideas on how today's couples are choosing to word their invitations.

Be sure to include information about your wedding dress code, if there is one. No one wants to arrive at a black-tie wedding in a suit or sport jacket.

Printing and Mailing

There are many lower-budget printing services that will print your invitations for much less than a stationery or wedding store would charge. Bridal magazines also have special reduced rates for subscribers.

♥

Order wedding announcements and thank you cards simultaneously to coordinate with your invitations.

♥

Nowadays, some couples even e-mail or fax their invitations. Casual can be chic! Be sure this choice fits your style, though. It may offend some more traditionally minded recipients.

♥

Envelopes can be hand-addressed if you have the time. This is typically more personal than affixing labels to each invitation.

♥

You can have your computer print your guests' addresses and your return address on the envelopes, but note that this can be incredibly time-consuming if you need to hand-feed the envelopes one by one.

♥

Use "Love" stamps or other pretty floral stamps on your invitations and reply cards for a romantic touch.

♥

Bring your invitations to the post office and take the time to hand-cancel the stamps on each instead of having the postal meter run a black line across the bottom of your invitations. It looks classier. Realize, however, that even if you have your envelopes hand-canceled, sometimes they still get double-canceled by the postal machines. Unfortunately, there is no way to prevent this.

♥

Some couples choose to use sealing wax on the back of the envelopes for a classy effect. Be aware, though, that these seals can crack or chip during handling by the postal service. Seals can also lead to delays in guests receiving their invitations because they can cause postal machines to jam and even tear your envelopes because of the uneven lumps that these waxes make.

♥

To avoid these problems, some couples use sealing wax on the inner envelopes of their invitations instead of the exposed outer envelope. (Don't use candle wax; it is too brittle and will crumble.) Be sure anything with wax seals (inside or out) is hand-canceled at the post office.

♥

Your Guest List

When compiling your guest list, decide whether you will include only the spouses of your guests, or whether you would like to invite fiancés and significant others as well.

•

If you address an invitation with the words "and guest," you should assume that the invitee will bring one. Factor this into the number of guests your budget, location, and caterer can accommodate, and decide as a couple what you would like to do.

•

You can always leave out the words "and guest" initially, then call your single guests closer to the actual wedding, once you have a firmer idea of how many people will be attending, and offer them the option to bring a date if they would like.

•

Send out your invitations six to eight weeks in advance. That way you'll have plenty of time for slower RSVPs as well as time to move to your "B" list if your numbers are coming in lower than expected.

•

Any international guests or those traveling great distances to attend should receive their invitations or, at minimum, information regarding the wedding, ten to twelve weeks in advance as a courtesy to assist them in travel planning.

•

Include a "reply by" date on your reply card to encourage guests to RSVP in a timely manner.

•

Prestamp your reply card as a courtesy to invitees.

•

Check with your caterer as to the absolute final date you can let him or her know your total number of guests. As this date approaches, if you have not heard from certain guests, you and the groom should call them to find out if they are planning to attend.

•

After the Wedding

Frame, matte, or etch your invitation on a silver serving tray, glass plate, or Lucite block to serve as a beautiful reminder of your special day.

5 ♥

Handling PWS, Part 1: Pre-Wedding Stress

Wedding planning can involve a lot of commotion and anxiety. Here are some helpful ideas that may take some of the stress out of things.

Nurturing Your Relationship

♥　♥　♥　♥　♥

Remember that this is *your* wedding: yours and your fiancé's, that is. Take some relaxing time together to celebrate your love.

•

Get away for the weekend.

•

Have a date night. Make that special time with a moratorium on wedding planning discussions. Talk about all of the things you used to talk about before your wedding was the main topic of conversation.

•

You and your fiancé may want to sign up for a cooking, athletic, or enrichment class to give yourselves a structured setting where wedding talk is forbidden and you can enjoy sharing a new experience together.

•

If you think you or your fiancé are getting cold feet, rest assured that this is normal. But be sure to talk about it with him.

•

Keep your sense of humor. Laugh about things. Whatever the problem, know that this too shall pass.

•

Focus on your love for each other and remind yourselves of the reasons you chose to marry one another.

•

Nurturing Yourself

♥   ♥   ♥   ♥   ♥

Breathe. Sometimes counting to ten and taking deep breaths can improve your day immensely.

Sign up for a yoga, meditation, aerobics, or other self-help class that gives you a chance to focus on yourself and get in touch with your true feelings. Just an hour a week for yourself can work wonders.

If you have trouble sleeping for days or months prior to your wedding because your mind is reeling, talk to your doctor about ways to relax yourself through breathing, medication, or other therapies. You don't want to arrive at the wedding with huge bags under your eyes.

Hiring a Wedding Consultant

♥   ♥   ♥   ♥   ♥

If work keeps you too busy or if your mother or in-laws are not a part of your wedding planning process, de-stress by hiring a wedding consultant to assist you in the planning process. This professional will have contacts in virtually every area related to weddings, from music to catering and even emotional counseling.

♥

It is worth it to spend the money on a coordinator, especially if you are getting married at your home or in a remote location that requires more extensive ceremony and reception preparation.

♥

Most hotels have an on-site coordinator who can assist you. The coordinator's services may already be included in the hotel's wedding package.

♥

If you hire a coordinator, be sure that you click with him or her. Your wedding day will be stressful (as is the planning process), so you want to be sure you can get along well.

♥

Dealing with Your In-Laws

♥   ♥   ♥   ♥   ♥

Let your fiancé be your middleman between you and your in-laws. If you have issues that involve them (for instance, the rehearsal dinner or mother-in-law stresses), have your fiancé be your go-between.

•

Because the planning process often involves heightened emotions and sticky issues such as who to invite or how much things cost, don't make the mistake of "snapping" at one of your in-laws. The wedding is about the two of you, but as the saying goes, "You don't marry the guy, you marry the family," so don't create too many waves that could build up into long-term grudges.

•

Dealing with
Relationship Stresses

♥   ♥   ♥   ♥   ♥

Communicate. Communicate. Communicate. Talk things over with your fiancé. He is the one person who should be able to truly and deeply understand, love, and support you during the planning process.

If your relationship with your fiancé worsens considerably after you two become engaged and you two cannot work things out on your own, consider seeking premarital counseling. Sometimes an objective third party who has no alliances with either of you can offer fresh insights and assistance.

Seeking professional help prior to your wedding is not an admission that your relationship is a failure. Rather, it shows your commitment to wanting to work things out together no matter what it takes.

Remember, a wedding ranks up there as one of life's most stressful events, so don't tackle your personal issues alone. Reach out for help.

Some couples want to have a prenuptial agreement. While creating this legal document can cause intense stress and negotiation between your lawyers, your families, and the two of you, try to stay a team throughout the process and keep all lines of communication wide open.

Once the document is signed and executed, forget about it, let go of any ill will that may have surfaced during the process, and move forward with the fun. After all, your wedding is really about your love, not your assets.

Your Support Group

♥   ♥   ♥   ♥   ♥

Take some time out with your mother, close girl-friends, or sister(s), and also with people who have been through the wedding process. Share your feelings with them, listen to their own stories of angst, and realize that you are not alone in the world.

♥

Your greatest support group may be somebody you meet in line at the grocery store who has been through a wedding before.

♥

If your parents are driving you nuts, you may want to consider venting to your siblings or close girlfriends before going to your fiancé. That way you'll be able to defuse some of your tension rather than laying it on him. After all, there is no reason to burden him with more of your own family's dirty laundry than is necessary.

♥

Ahead of time, delegate to your maid of honor and other wedding attendants such duties as making phone calls, helping you address and stamp wedding invitations, or coordinating the fittings for the bridesmaids' dresses.

♥

Research and Organization

♥   ♥   ♥   ♥   ♥

Be organized! Get a wedding planner or a three-ring binder with dividers and pockets to keep all of your receipts, research, contracts, and ideas so that you can always access things in one portable place.

●

Collect wedding-related materials from friends. If you are worrying about writing your wedding program or letter to out-of-town guests, ask other married friends for copies of theirs to use as models. There is no need to reinvent the wheel when there are lots of resources out there!

●

Read, read, read: wedding books, magazines, and Web sites. There is an abundance of information available on virtually every wedding-related topic imaginable.

●

When reading wedding-related literature, use a high-lighter and self-stick flags to mark areas and ideas that are specific to your needs, questions, or concerns. That way the stacks of books, magazines, and other wedding-related paperwork won't overwhelm you.

•

Wedding-Day Suggestions

♥   ♥   ♥   ♥   ♥

Make time to see your fiancé on the day of your wedding. Even if you don't want him to see you in your dress before the wedding, meet for breakfast or just for a smooch and a hug. Connect with him on the day of the wedding in some way and your jitters will ease. Chances are you are used to seeing each other every day, so start your wedding day with at least a great hello. There are no rules against that!

Have specific duties assigned to your maid of honor and attendants that will ease the tension on your big day. For instance, your maid of honor should be on hand to help you bustle your dress, go to the restroom (which can be a difficult task in a wedding gown!), and change into your going-away outfit. She also can be responsible for your checklists, speeches, and Bride's Survival Kit (see chapter 1).

Then sit back, relax, and enjoy. Try to let all of your planning fall into place, and know that pretty much everything from here on is out of your hands.

Have faith that all of your hard work, decisions and planning will pay off. Just remember, anything that goes wrong should be laughed at and will make for the best stories after the fact.

✳

6

Doing It YOUR Way: Modern Twists on Traditional Weddings

Weddings of the new millennium have no hard-and-fast rules. The number of completely traditional weddings—with the typical church, hall, and reception format—has decreased dramatically as family geographic limitations, mixed marriages, blended families, and second weddings have become more prevalent. Today's couples get married on live television, atop mountains, in theme parks, and even under water. Whether or not you are daring enough to be this extreme, you'll enjoy these fun ideas for how to have a traditional wedding and still incorporate modern twists.

Location, Officiant, and Vows

♥   ♥   ♥   ♥   ♥

Consider using an alternative site for your wedding, such as a museum, an aquarium, a clifftop, a historic mansion, a boat, a baseball field, a beach, a ranch, or even the zoo. The sky's the limit! (For more unusual locations, see chapter 8.)

•

Instead of using a priest, rabbi, or judge as your officiant, have a close friend marry you: perhaps the person who introduced the two of you, a significant family friend, or even a member of your wedding party. Ask a wedding coordinator, do research on the Web, or check with your justice of the peace about the requirements for becoming a wedding officiant in your state. In most states, your officiant can obtain a certificate that is legally valid to lead your ceremony.

•

One couple happened to love dinosaurs, so their friend who officiated read from a children's book about dinosaurs and taped the words of his ceremony inside.

•

Write your own vows (see chapter 10). The words of love that you exchange can include poetry, music, and personal anecdotes in addition to, or instead of, the traditional "to have and to hold from this day forward for as long as you both shall live."

•

When writing your own vows, be careful not to include too many inside jokes that none of the guests will understand. The ceremony is not the time for this.

•

Wedding Quilts, Scrapbooks, and Ketubahs
♥   ♥   ♥   ♥   ♥

Mail all the wedding guests a small piece of fabric several months before the wedding, with instructions to decorate it with a permanent message or image. For a Jewish wedding, the fabric pieces can be stitched together into a marriage canopy (or chuppah) that you and your groom stand under during the ceremony.

For a non-Jewish wedding, the fabric pieces can be made into a bridal quilt that will be a beautiful and personal keepsake to hang on the wall of your new home or to use at the end of your bed.

An alternative to this idea is to send a piece of beautiful paper to all the guests beforehand and have them inscribe a message to the newly engaged couple: a piece of advice, a poem, or a thought about marriage. These thoughts can then be put into an album or scrapbook for the guests to peruse at the sign-in table.

For Jewish weddings, have your ketubah (marriage contract) designed by an artist instead of using a traditional document completed by the rabbi. You and your fiancé can work together to add symbols significant to your relationship. Later, you can hang the ketubah in your bedroom as a permanent reminder of the commitment you two have made.

One couple designed a travel-theme ketubah with painted images of landmarks of places they had visited together, while another incorporated meaningful quotes, colors, and other symbols of their love. Be sure to display the ketubah prominently on an easel at the reception for guests to view.

Programs, Guest Books, and Beyond

♥   ♥   ♥   ♥   ♥

Wedding programs have become a popular way to make all the guests feel included in the ceremony. You and your fiancé can print a personal message in the program as well as list the names of the wedding party members and other participants and your relationship to them. Religious or cultural wedding traditions can also be described succinctly in the program.

♥

Print in your programs or announce prior to the wedding that guests should turn off their cell phones, beepers, and watch alarms so as not to disrupt key moments of the wedding.

♥

Have some other items for people to view at the guest book sign-in table, such as pictures of the two of you, a poster with fun snapshots from your relationship mounted on it, or even framed photos of your parents and grandparents on their wedding days. While waiting to sign in, guests can look at these happy images.

♥

As an alternative to a guest book, mount an enlargement of your engagement photo or wedding invitation and have guests sign it with a silver or gold pen as they enter the wedding.

♥

Make a wedding banner with your names and wedding date for guests to sign with permanent markers at the wedding or rehearsal dinner. It will be a special keepsake from your big day.

♥

The Ceremony

♥   ♥   ♥   ♥   ♥

More and more couples are choosing to have both their mothers and their fathers walk them down the aisle to "give them away."

•

One bride arranged to hook up her laptop computer to a video camera at the wedding so her out-of-town friends who were unable to make the wedding could attend the ceremony virtually.

•

Many brides and grooms also choose to walk part of the way down the aisle alone to symbolize their independence from their parents.

•

Walk down the aisle to something other than classical music, and exit the ceremony to a song other than the wedding march. A rock and roll or other popular song offers an upbeat twist.

•

Have the flower girl drop rose petals as she walks down the aisle. One bride saved and dried the petals from the roses her groom had given her at their engagement, and gave them to her flower girl to scatter in this way.

•

Instead of having the ring bearer carry a pillow with the rings attached, consider using something more personal to your relationship, such as a baseball glove (if you two met at a game or are big fans) or another special symbol of your love.

•

Or use a homemade ring pillow made from beautiful handkerchiefs that belonged to your grandmother, great-aunt, or other older relative. Stitch these family heirlooms together and stuff the pillow with feathers or scented potpourri.

•

There is no rule stating that the bride and groom must face the officiant and turn their backs on the guests for the duration of the ceremony. Instead, turn toward your guests and have the officiant stand alongside you (or with his or her back to the audience). This personal touch makes guests feel that they are a more intimate part of your wedding, because they can witness your expressions and your love for each other.

•

If you are lighting a unity candle in your ceremony, have one made with extra wicks to allow your children to participate in this part of the wedding. What a beautiful way to reflect the blending of your new family with this special symbol!

●

During some wedding ceremonies, the couple shares a cup of wine at the altar. (Just be sure that it is white wine, so there's no chance of accidental stains!) You and your groom can each be given your own glass of wine and then together pour it into one larger cup, so you can both share sips from the same glass.

●

A new trend known as a rose exchange is popping into ceremonies. A single red or white rose is exchanged as a first gift between the bride and groom to symbolize their love for each other. The couple then exchanges a rose in a special location in their new home on each anniversary or significant highlight in their marriage, reminding them of the vows they exchanged and the promises they made on their wedding day.

●

If yours is a marriage that blends families, include your children in the ceremony and vows. Exchange personal vows with them as well. Giving them a ring or other token will make them feel special. One couple gave their eight-year-old daughter a tiny diamond ring at the rehearsal dinner so that she could proudly wear it to the wedding.

●

At the end of the traditional Jewish wedding ceremony, the groom breaks a glass with his foot. For a more egalitarian ceremony, some couples choose to break the glass together or to have two glasses, one for each person to break.

●

If you are getting married in a church, arrange to have the church bells ring at the moment you kiss and are pronounced man and wife. It is a dramatic touch.

●

If you are not getting married in a church but want the church bell effect, you can give guests a tiny bell tied with a white satin ribbon to ring at the conclusion of the ceremony as you and your new spouse walk down the aisle.

●

Instead of throwing rice (or the more ecologically correct birdseed) at the end of a wedding, consider tossing rose petals or confetti, releasing balloons or butterflies (if outdoors), or having tiny bottles of bubbles for guests to blow at you.

●

Some couples even release white doves at the end of the ceremony to symbolize the couple's love, faithfulness, and peace. (These are specially trained homing pigeons that you can essentially rent to use at your ceremony. Consult your yellow pages or local bridal directories for these special services.)

●

Other unique touches that are becoming popular to incorporate into traditional weddings include fireworks displays, skywriting, or airplanes flying overhead with banner messages. The sky's literally the limit!

●

Consider having a special song that is meaningful to you and your fiancé played or sung during the ceremony.

●

Wedding books and consultants will offer ideas or mandates on everything, from specific ways to proceed down the aisle to the spot where you should stand for the ceremony. Remember, though, that this is *your* wedding and that you are allowed to bend the rules to accommodate your desires.

•

The Reception

♥   ♥   ♥   ♥   ♥

At the beginning of the reception, when the married couple is announced and members of the wedding party are introduced, instead of a drum roll or cheesy music, consider having the DJ or band play the theme from *Rocky* as you enter.

Other fun songs that can jazz things up include the *Tonight Show* theme song; Queen's *Another One Bites the Dust* or *We Are the Champions; Celebration; Rock-n-Roll Part 2* (a sports event/group participation song); the theme from *Star Wars, Jaws,* or *Indiana Jones;* the fight song from your alma mater; or any other song that is upbeat and meaningful to you both.

Whenever wedding guests clink their glasses, the bride and groom are supposed to kiss. Many couples put a twist on this tradition by finding out who started the clinking and making them kiss their date. One couple had pink (female) and blue (male) balloons prefilled with air and a guest's name: if clinking occurred, one pink and on blue balloon were popped and those guests had to kiss. This new tradition incorporated and embarrassed everyone (and also cut down greatly on the clinking!)

Alternatively, the balloons can contain messages or trivia questions about the bride and groom, which the guests will have to answer when clinking occurs.

One couple had a movie screen lowered and projected on it a short slide show accompanied by the words of a love song displayed karaoke-style, so that guests could sing along.

My own lifelong friend and angelic-voiced bridesmaid sang during the dance portion of our reception, which was very special.

A Final Thought

After the wedding and honeymoon, print your vows on pretty paper, and then frame and hang them somewhere in your new home where you two can glance at them and remind yourselves of the promises you exchanged.

7

Unique Wedding Locations

With couples getting married later in life as well as more than one million people a year planning second marriages, destination weddings are fast becoming a unique, cost-effective alternative to traditional weddings. A destination wedding is just that: getting married at a destination (other than your home), such as Mexico, Europe, or an attractive domestic locale like Hawaii. Additionally, getting married at home offers an intimate setting, often with a personal touch and special significance to the bride or groom. At-home weddings can also be more cost effective by eliminating the need for a site fee.

Destination Weddings

♥　　♥　　♥　　♥　　♥

Destination weddings are more cost effective than traditional weddings, since they tend to be more intimate and involve fewer guests. Since you and your new spouse will already be at your honeymoon destination following the wedding, there is also no need for extra airfare or transportation. Destination weddings generally cost about one-third as much as traditional weddings.

•

Guests will enjoy planning a vacation around your wedding weekend, so a trip to an exotic place like the Caribbean or Hawaii makes for a more dramatic way to celebrate your marriage.

•

Many hotels offer destination wedding packages that may include free nights at their property or other perks for the bridal couple. Some even offer room discounts to wedding guests. Often the services of a wedding coordinator are included in the package as well.

•

Check with the hotel where you plan to wed as to the different levels of their packages. The price can increase greatly as you add on different perks to your ceremony and reception.

•

The wedding coordinator at your hotel can often arrange for beachside, clifftop, boat, or even hot-air balloon locations. One couple in Hawaii exchanged vows on the peak of a volcano, atop donkeys.

•

The guest list at your destination wedding can be as short or long as you choose. You two can be the only attendees and your hotel's wedding coordinator can provide you with witnesses, or you can have as many guests as you like who are willing to travel to your destination.

•

Destination weddings are ideal for second marriages or those that include blended families. They are also excellent alternatives for the busy working couple who does not have time to plan all of the details. If you want to leave everything up to the hotel's wedding coordinator, he or she can arrange it all.

•

Sandals and other all-inclusive hotel chains offer special packages for couples who get married at one of their resorts. For instance, Weddingmoons at Sandals offers free honeymoons as well as other newlywed perks for couples who say "I do" there. Consult your travel agent or the property directly for more information on these and other offers.

•

Consider incorporating local traditions and flavor into your destination wedding. For example, Hawaiian weddings can include such elements as hula dancers, conch shell blowers, outrigger canoe transportation, and Hawaiian music and food. A raucous luau may also suit your style.

•

If you get married in Mexico, cliff divers, native dancers and musicians, and fiesta decorations can enhance your wedding.

•

If you are getting married in a country that is not your own, or if you are a widow or a divorcée, check in advance with the consulate, the American Embassy in that region, or your hotel's wedding coordinator for any requirements that you may need to address prior to your wedding. Some places have marriage laws that require a blood test, proof of divorce or decease, or short waiting periods (usually twenty-four to forty-eight hours) during which brides and grooms have to "reside" in the area before they are eligible to get married there.

•

Also be sure that your marriage will be recognized in your state of residence once you return home by checking with your local marriage bureau or justice of the peace.

•

Other unique locations for destination weddings include a winery, a farm, an art museum, a sculpture garden, the quadrangle or church of your alma mater, the roof or top floor of a building, a historic landmark, a racetrack, a ski slope, a basketball court, a botanical garden or lakeside, a movie studio or theater, or your own or a close relative's home (more on that below).

•

When choosing a unique wedding site, keep in mind any logistical difficulties that the location may pose, such as accessible parking or transportation issues, the number of people the space will accommodate, hiring help to assist at the site, table and chair rentals, insurance coverage, climate issues, and so on.

•

At-Home Weddings

♥   ♥   ♥   ♥   ♥

Getting married at home offers a more personal and intimate locale than a church hall or hotel ballroom by virtue of it being at home.

Imagine tossing your bouquet or garter from the same balcony or patio where you also shared special childhood memories.

If you have any unique childhood pictures (for example, you playing dress-up bride and walking down the staircase), put them out for people to see—it will add that special magic of getting married at home.

If you are planning an at-home wedding at your or your groom's home or at the home of parents or in-laws, it is a good idea to hire a wedding coordinator to assist with the hundreds of unforeseen complications that may arise. A coordinator will more than earn his or her fee in helping you with these issues.

Realize that while there is no site fee involved in getting married at home, you may incur additional costs to rent things such as tables and chairs, a dance floor, and restroom facilities for the wedding staff.

If your wedding ceremony or reception is being held outdoors, consider the costs of supplemental lighting, heat lamps if the event is in the evening, tents in case of rain, umbrellas for the valets to use when ushering guests from their cars to the site, and so on.

In addition to wanting everything you rent and purchase for the wedding and reception to look nice, you'll also want the grounds of your host's home to look presentable. Gardening maintenance, upkeep of greenery, and perhaps even the planting of additional flowers to complement your centerpieces can add hundreds or thousands of dollars of unexpected costs.

Don't feel the need to be excessive, however, by decorating the garden or trees with ribbons, fabric, or extra rickrack. Let the beauty of the outdoors be just that: natural beauty.

Caterers often do not have enough room to prepare food for guests in a home kitchen; they usually require additional space, such as an entire garage, where they can set up their burners, refrigeration units, coffeepots, food assembly line, and other essentials. Be prepared.

Strangers—such as the hired help of the caterers, the photographer, and musicians—will have access to your host's home. Be certain that all wedding staff is fully insured and that the home is insured.

Consider purchasing wedding insurance for the day of the event to protect you and your host from unforeseen weather conditions, damages to personal property, or even theft from the home. Or have the host add umbrella insurance to his or her homeowner's insurance policy to cover this.

Parking can also be a critical issue for at-home weddings. You will likely need to hire valets or organize shuttle bus service from local parking lots. Check with your town hall or police department to see if there are any parking limitations or zoning concerns in your area.

Neighbors can become disgruntled and unhappy with the noise, traffic, and wear and tear that your wedding may create on your street. To defuse any bombs, personally deliver flyers to your neighbors in advance seeking their cooperation for this special one-time event. One bride delivered teddy bear–shaped chocolates to each neighbor, asking them to "bear with us" during the wedding event.

Check with your local police department about any noise ordinances or curfews in your town that you may not be aware of. Nothing would be worse than unknowingly breaking the law and having your wedding or reception halted by the police.

Talk with your musicians in advance about the decibel level of their amplifiers, to ensure that they will be able to soften their music if the reception continues until the wee hours.

Try to reuse the chairs from your ceremony, as well as any other rented items you may have, at the reception. Note, however, that while this recycling may cut costs, hired help may still be required to assist in transporting these items.

8

Off the Beaten Path: Holiday and Theme Weddings

Weddings are getting more imaginative by the minute. Saying "I do" on a holiday or creating a theme wedding are popular trends. A wedding organized around a theme can be as creative and over-the-top as you choose, incorporating decorations, foods, costumes, music, and other accents related to the theme. Or the theme can be woven in more subtly, as a common thread that is carried throughout the event. Possible themes include a time period, a season, a color, a dance style, or the couple's favorite hobby or pastime.

If you two would like to have a wedding with some off-beat or ultra-creative twists, the following ideas may both inspire you and demonstrate that your options for having a unique wedding are truly limitless. Many second-wedding brides and grooms are particularly interested in exploring these alternative trends, since they have already experienced a traditional wedding. Have fun!

Holiday Weddings

♥   ♥   ♥   ♥   ♥

Holidays are popular dates to get married. It's often easier for your guests to take off work at these times, and they make for even more festive celebrations.

•

Getting married on a holiday assures you that your future anniversaries will not be forgotten!

•

Be aware that holidays can pose problems for guests who have their own annual tradition of celebrating with family or friends. Some guests may not be able to attend your wedding because of these limitations. On the other hand, a holiday wedding may be preferable if you are having a smaller event or want to limit the number of people who attend.

•

Holidays on which many couples get married are Labor Day weekend, Memorial Day weekend, and Fourth of July weekend. This list is not all inclusive, however. More and more couples are choosing New Year's Eve, Valentine's Day, Christmas, Thanksgiving, or Halloween as festive alternatives.

•

A New Year's Eve wedding might include noise-makers or a fireworks display, and can even be timed to have a countdown to your final kiss or "I do" at midnight. Guests can also come in masquerade or wear black tie to a New Year's Eve wedding.

•

Valentine's Day weddings offer the option to indulge in romantic touches: red and white roses, sexier bridesmaid dresses, hearts galore, cupids, and other romance-related items.

•

Halloween weddings may include guests arriving in costume, haunted houses, and creative centerpieces complete with dried ice, spider webs, ghoulish music, and trick-or-treating for party favors. The couple can come as Frankenstein and his bride or as members of the Addams Family. "The Monster Mash" and "Thriller" are popular tunes to play at the reception, and a pumpkin-pie wedding cake could be fun, too.

•

Theme Weddings
♥   ♥   ♥   ♥   ♥
Popular Time-Period Themes

For a Renaissance/courtly wedding, invitations are sent on scrolls and the groom arrives as a knight in shining armor atop a horse. Entertainment can include a jester and court dancers, and the setting could be a castle, château, or ballroom decorated like an Old English inn.

At a Roaring '20s wedding, guests come in costume, members of the wedding party dress as flappers or men of the mob, the DJ teaches guests the Charleston, and the newlyweds drive off in an antique car.

In a '50s theme wedding, female attendants wear bobby socks and poodle skirts and male attendants sport letterman sweaters or leather jackets. A milkshake bar or soda fountain, Elvis and sock hop music or a jukebox, and '50s memorabilia can add to the ambiance. Serve food that you would find at a diner, such as burgers, fries, and egg creams.

A disco/'70s-era wedding can be fun (if you have the guts!). The groom and groomsmen could wear ruffled shirts and polyester tuxedoes and the bridal party could dress in platform shoes, tube tops, and bell bottoms. Add a disco ball and colored lights, *Saturday Night Fever* music, and Afros and big feathered hairdos.

Other time-period themes include medieval, colonial, or caveman.

Other Themes

For a nautical theme wedding, invitations can be designed to resemble tickets for a cruise or boat ride. The bride and groom can dress as the captain and first mate, while their attendants can be pirates, sailors, or the crew. Seafood and sushi would be fun fare to serve, with centerpieces of live goldfish, floating toy boats, starfish, or shells. Instead of numbers, table assignments could use shipyard or seafaring terms such as port, starboard, tack, jibe, rudder, or compass.

♥

Luau, Hawaiian, or island theme weddings have become popular, too. Guests are welcomed with leis. Hula skirts and Hawaiian shirts are the attendants' garb. The ambiance is enhanced with Hawaiian music, foods, and entertainment, tiki torches, and table assignments that use the names of islands or exotic plants. For the centerpieces, consider either clear bowls with floating tropical flowers, candles, seashells, and sand, or fishbowls filled with colored coral and goldfish. Fun wedding favors could be shell-shaped chocolates or seashells painted with the couple's names and wedding date.

♥

A movie, television, or entertainment theme wedding could require guests to come dressed in the spirit of the couple's favorite TV show or film such as *The Brady Bunch*, *Star Wars*, or a classic movie. Invitations designed to resemble a movie placard, playbill, or tickets to a show are a fun touch. Theme music and food from the TV show or film can add to the ambiance, and fun memorabilia from it can decorate the space. Party favors such as chocolates shaped like televisions or director's megaphones are also unique.

♥

Sports theme weddings can be set at a sports arena, baseball stadium, racetrack, or football field. The bride can throw the first pitch or the groom can literally kick off the ceremony. One couple walked through an archway of attendants holding up baseball bats. Peanuts and popcorn can be served during the ceremony, and baseball hats printed with the couple's names and wedding date can be clever favors.

♥

Extreme weddings are also becoming a trend. Couples have exchanged vows on roller coasters, atop observation platforms at national monuments, while bungee jumping or sky diving, in airplanes or hot-air balloons, underwater while clad in scuba gear, and even on motorcycles with their Harley Davidson buddies. No idea is impossible or too wild.

♥

Eco-weddings, or environmentally friendly weddings, are often held outdoors, under natural light, with energy and conservation in mind. All aspects of these events are "green," from the birdseed thrown at the end of the ceremony to the organic foods served at the reception.

♥

Mystery weddings invite guests to a murder mystery event, during which games are played that culminate in a wedding. Often the actual wedding is a surprise to the invited guests!

♥

Surprise weddings invite guests to an event that eventually becomes a wedding. Family reunions or holidays are good occasions for these.

♥

Walt Disney World weddings are true fairytale weddings that can be planned with any Disney theme possibility imaginable. Mickey and Minnie can visit or serve as officiants; the bride can dress as Cinderella and be chauffeured to the ball to meet her handsome prince in a pumpkin-shaped horse-drawn carriage; couples can even exchange vows on selected Magic Kingdom rides.

Contact Walt Disney World in Orlando, Florida, directly for more information.

♥

Las Vegas isn't just a place for spur-of-the-moment elopements anymore. Every theme hotel offers unique packages, from the traditional to the adventurous. Say "I do" atop a replica of the Eiffel Tower (it is much cheaper than flying to Paris!), aboard a pirate ship at Treasure Island, on a gondola at the Venetian, in a Renaissance ceremony at the Excalibur, in a replica of Elvis's Graceland Chapel with an Elvis impersonator as your minister, or in many other uniquely Vegas ways! Contact hotels directly or the Las Vegas Tourism Office for more information.

♥

For the ultimate wedding thrill-seekers only: Say "I do" on the world's highest roller coaster, atop the Stratosphere tower in Las Vegas. If you two want your relationship to reach new heights, why not get hitched on the highest point in the western United States?

♥

9

Wedding Budget

Nowadays the parents of the bride are not always the exclusive financial backers of the wedding. In-laws may contribute, close family and friends sometimes do, and often the bride and groom assume most or all of the costs associated with the big day. With second weddings, the couple is almost always solely responsible for all the costs. So it's not surprising that more and more couples are interested in budget weddings.

When some of us hear the word "budget," we automatically associate it with being cheap, but this does not have to be the case. Below you'll find money-saving ideas that won't cheapen the ambiance of your events.

Planning, Budgeting, and Research

♥ ♥ ♥ ♥ ♥

When you consider your wedding budget, sit down with your fiancé and discuss the elements of a wedding that mean the most to you. Then focus the bulk of your funds on the most meaningful items.

●

Spend money on the parts of your wedding that you will really remember and cherish after it is all over. The wedding day ends in a flash, but the pictures will last forever. So you may not want to skimp on your photographer.

●

Set up a wedding budget for yourself on your computer with a spreadsheet or similar program. Or go online and visit wedding Web sites. Many of them have programs with wedding budget planners that may assist you in staying on target and within your means. Quicken or Microsoft Excel spreadsheets work well, too.

●

Set up a separate checking account for your wedding expenses. It will help you keep track of your costs and separate them out from your everyday expenditures.

●

If you plan to make purchases for members of your wedding party, such as bridesmaids' shoes or groomsmen's tuxedo deposits, pay with a credit card. That way, if anything goes wrong with sizes or colors, you'll have recourse through the credit card company (even if the store has a "no cancellation" or "no return" policy).

•

Attend local wedding expos when they come to your town or a city nearby. While the vendors can be aggressive and the crowds sometimes overwhelming, an abundance of fun ideas, discounts, and free prizes, including honeymoons, reception sites, and limousine transportation, are raffled off.

•

Spend time in the wedding aisle of your local library or bookstore. Read as many books as you can, and jot down ideas that excite you. Buy only the books that seem right for you (especially this one!), and review the chapters on money-saving ideas.

•

Saving on the Dress

♥   ♥   ♥   ♥   ♥

Buy a simple, flattering white dress in the women's clothing section of a department store or boutique. Use this as the basis for a gown that you or a seamstress can detail with lace, beading, and other finery. You'll spend a fraction of the cost and will have a totally unique dress!

Consignment stores, discount warehouses, and renting are all less expensive alternatives to buying a full-priced dress from a retailer or salon.

Veils can also be borrowed or rented.

Many brides are designing their own gowns with special touches that accentuate their body type. These custom gowns can often be more cost effective than those bought off the rack.

Some brides redesign or alter their mother's, sister's, or close friend's gown.

Remember that you don't have to wear the dress only once.

Time and Place

♥   ♥   ♥   ♥   ♥

Have your wedding at an off-peak time of year or on an off day. June, September, and December are the most popular months for weddings, and weekends and national holidays are the most expensive days of the week to get married.

♥

Brunches and buffets are typically less expensive than dinners or evening events.

♥

Get married in a nontraditional location such as a public school auditorium, an empty movie theater, a friend's home, or the beach. The ceremony site fees will be significantly lower, if there is any charge at all. (Beware, though: Costs associated with receptions at these locales may be higher than you anticipate since the cost of equipment, tables, chairs, servers, and permits may add up.)

♥

Keep your wedding party small—maybe just family only—to limit complexities and expenses related to attendants.

♥

Elope, have a civil ceremony, or plan a destination wedding. Then celebrate afterward with family and friends at a reception. This is much more cost effective than a full-blown wedding.

♥

Invitations and Guests

♥　♥　♥　♥　♥

Make your own invitations by hand or on the computer.

●

Hand-address invitations or run the envelopes through your computer instead of hiring a calligrapher.

●

If you choose to get invitations printed, don't have them engraved; just serigraph them.

●

If you and your fiancé agree to limit your guest list, do not include the names of your friends' boyfriends or girlfriends on the envelopes. Some couples have an "engaged- or married-only" rule; all other guests are considered single and are expected to attend alone.

●

Don't invite children to the wedding unless it is imperative. You'll save on costs here, too.

•

Register at a travel agency so guests can contribute toward your honeymoon, enabling you to free up money to put toward your wedding.

•

Flowers and Alternatives

♥   ♥   ♥   ♥   ♥

Instead of elaborate ribbons, tulle, and flower bundles, consider having the bridesmaids' bouquets be fresh-cut flowers wrapped with a simple satin ribbon.

One bride had an usher give a single flower to each guest sitting closest to the aisle before the ceremony began. As the bride walked down the aisle, she literally collected her bouquet from her guests, who participated in making it, and the maid of honor then bundled and tied all the flowers together for her.

Consider using silk flowers for your bouquets or centerpieces. They can be prepared far in advance, and you don't have to worry about them wilting at the reception.

Look into renting pre-made floral centerpieces that can be used one time for a fraction of the cost of fresh flowers.

Many brides save by ordering flowers and arrangements through their local grocery store or wholesaler such as Costco, Price Club, or Sam's Club. You may be pleasantly surprised by how nice the arrangements are.

When the ceremony is over, reuse the loose cut flowers from the bridesmaids' bouquets by putting them into prepared fresh-water vases to serve as the centerpieces for the reception.

Reuse and recycle whatever you can.

The flowers that decorate the site of the ceremony can be reused if they are transported to the reception.

Cost-effective alternatives to floral centerpieces include balloons, confetti, or potted plants; baskets of fresh fruit, gourds, and autumn leaves (if seasonal); pretty tissues, fabric squares, or gift wrap; flat circular mirrors with votives arranged on top; or a few pictures of the bride and groom in fun scenarios, arranged in a circle facing the guests.

Candles and votives should be used everywhere, from on the tables to around the reception area. They are much less costly than fresh flowers and create a classy ambiance.

Wedding Favors

♥   ♥   ♥   ♥   ♥

Make your own wedding favors and accessories. Arts and crafts stores have many inexpensive trinkets, beads, lace, sequins, and pearls. They even carry small figurines that can be painted to go atop your wedding cake or in centerpieces. If you have creative friends or family members, enlist their help!

♥

Other inexpensive homemade wedding party favors include painted napkin rings with your names and wedding date, cookies, fudge or chocolates wrapped in tissue or clear cellophane with ribbon, or tiny potted plants.

♥

One bride made her table number plaques at a paint-your-own ceramics studio. She used 2- by 2-inch ceramic tiles, and on the front painted the table number (using different designs on each one: hearts, plaids, etc.). On the back, she printed the couple's names and wedding date. She had the ceramics store drill two holes at the top of each tile, and then strung organza ribbon through them and hung them from the centerpieces.

♥

If you choose to have table numbers assigned as opposed to open seating, consider having a large chart with all guests listed on it and their table number next to their names. This way, you save on the cost and confusion of individual table and place cards.

♥

Instead of the typical Jordan almonds wrapped in tulle, some couples give guests a packet of flower seeds with their names and wedding date attached; guests can plant them at their homes in honor of the wedding.

♥

Professional Services

♥   ♥   ♥   ♥   ♥

If you need items such as a wedding dress, veil, or garter, borrow them from friends and family instead of buying or renting them. If you need yarmulkes, borrow them from your local temple.

•

Have your makeup done for free at a department store counter the morning of the wedding. (Try out the artist first and consider tipping her afterward. Be sure she will be working the day of your wedding, too.)

•

Do your own hair and makeup, or have a family member do it for you (a trusted family member).

•

Use prerecorded classical music for your procession down the aisle and back, or have a single pianist rather than a string quartet.

•

Hire a DJ instead of a live band for your reception.

•

Save on a DJ by loading preselected songs into your computer and playing them at the reception. One bride asked her guests to request their favorite song on the reply card to the wedding, so many of the guests heard something they liked.

•

If you have no money in your budget to videotape your wedding, try calling the audiovisual department at a local high school or community college and hire a student to tape your wedding. These student-produced videos can have loads of fun effects, music, and audio, and they're often as good as a professional video. The same method could be used to find a photographer.

•

Or hire a professional photographer, but also see if close friends, family, or a photography student would be willing to take candid pictures with their own or throwaway cameras. You will be surprised to find that some of their pictures will be even better than the professional's, and at a fraction of the cost.

•

Reception

♥   ♥   ♥   ♥   ♥

If you would like to save time and money on your reception (meaning fewer hours to pay the band, photographer, videographer, and so on), then eliminate some of the less essential traditions, such as the garter throw or bouquet toss, if those activities are not as important to you.

Some brides choose to simply give their bouquet to the couple in attendance who have been married the longest as opposed to doing the traditional bouquet toss.

Have open seating without place cards or table assignments. This will save time, money, and headaches in planning.

One bride hired a local troop leader and six Girl Scouts to assist with serving and cleaning up at her reception. Since it was an hors d'oeuvres and light-fare event, their work mainly consisted of making sure platters were filled or replaced and keeping paper goods and supplies on the tables. The Girl Scouts got badges for donating their time, and the bride made a donation to the troop (which cost her much less than it would have to hire professional catering staff to do the same work).

Beverages

Use the table wine for toasts instead of purchasing champagne in addition.

♥

Consider a cash bar in lieu of offering alcoholic beverages.

♥

Find out if your establishment charges per bottle or per drink to guesstimate what your beverage costs will be.

♥

Check to see if you can bring in your own wine and liquor as opposed to using the reception hall's supplier. You may be charged a corkage fee per bottle, but this still might be more cost effective.

♥

Be sure that you will not be charged per head for alcoholic beverages for guests who are under legal drinking age. Have an accurate count of minors to provide to the catering or beverage manager.

♥

Advise servers not to refill wine glasses at tables until they are completely empty or unless a guest so requests. Many half-full glasses get refilled only to be left untouched.

♥

See if you can get a local college student to tend bar for you. Many universities actually offer bartending courses for students looking to make money on the side, and students may be less expensive than the on-site staff.

♥

If you choose to go with a student, make sure they will be insured, and also find out if they have bar supplies that they can use through their school or through a subcontracted catering company.

♥

Have water pitchers and wine bottles placed on the tables so guests can serve themselves.

♥

Consider skipping the cocktail hour altogether, and save on the alcohol and hors d'oeuvres.

♥

If you have a buffet, place a few wine bottles on each table so guests can serve themselves and save you the expense of hiring extra servers.

♥

If you do a champagne toast, instruct the servers to fill glasses only halfway. No one ever finishes the champagne, and this can cut your champagne bill in half.

♥

Desserts and Cake

♥   ♥   ♥   ♥   ♥

If you are paying for a set menu, see if you can eliminate the cost of the dessert and simply use your wedding cake as the sole dessert.

•

Consider serving a wedding cake baked at a grocery store or by a private baker who works out of his or her home. You can save hundreds of dollars, and the cake will actually taste pretty good!

•

Taking Off

♥   ♥   ♥   ♥   ♥

Don't change into a going-away outfit or even purchase a special one. Rather, exit as you entered: as the glowing bride.

Instead of a limousine, hire a town car or have a friend with a fun convertible or antique-looking car drive you and your spouse off after the ceremony. Or eliminate the drive off altogether and simply leave the wedding reception and head straight down the hotel hall to the honeymoon suite.

The joyous pleasure of being newlyweds on your honeymoon is a total high. Consider splurging on an exceptional honeymoon that you'll both appreciate.

10 ♥♥♥

Toasts, Roasts, and Writing Your Own Vows

Speaking at the shower, rehearsal dinner, bachelor or bachelorette party, and reception is an important way for wedding participants to share their feelings about the bride and groom, as well as to introduce both poignant and humorous anecdotes about them to the other guests. Many people speak publicly at the rehearsal dinner, wedding ceremony, and reception. This chapter speaks to most anyone who plans to share words about the happy couple—including parents, friends, wedding party members, and others. The bride and groom also give toasts to their parents, extended family, friends, and often each other.

Writing your own vows to exchange during the wedding ceremony is a meaningful way to personalize your love for one another in the presence of family and friends. Your vows are also a public testimony of your commitment to one another.

Toasts and Roasts
♥   ♥   ♥   ♥   ♥
By the Bride and Groom

More and more brides are giving toasts at their rehearsal dinner and reception. Typically, the rehearsal dinner toast is dedicated to the in-laws, bridesmaids, and any out-of-town guests who have traveled great distances to share in the celebration.

●

Grooms should be prepared to say a few words at the rehearsal dinner, too. In fact, the bride and groom may choose to do a joint toast to their parents and in-laws at the prenuptial event.

●

At the wedding, brides are now toasting their grooms in special tributes and reflecting on highlights of their relationship. Brides also toast their family and friends who contributed time and energy to the wedding.

●

Tell your fiancé in advance if you plan to say a few words to him at the reception. That way he can be prepared to return the gesture (rather than be embarrassed).

●

If you choose to toast at your reception, have extra copies of your speech in your maid of honor's possession. Also, remember that many contributors can be thanked in notes after the wedding, so save your toast for the most important people.

•

When considering what to say in your toast, roast, or speech, try to incorporate real, memorable anecdotes about the person you are honoring. These stories are great nuggets for guests and help them learn more about your special relationship with the honoree.

•

Your toast should not include too many inside jokes that only the person you are talking about will understand; many guests will feel left out and uncomfortable.

•

By Others

At the rehearsal dinner or reception, be careful if referring to the bride or groom's past relationships or telling stories involving their previous significant others. This can be hurtful and embarrassing for the couple. Better to save these types of reflections for guys- or girls-only bachelor or bachelorette parties or showers. Be tasteful at the big events.

There is a huge difference between a well-planned, well-thought-out best man speech and a drunken, fly-by-the-seat-of-your-pants roast. Think long and hard about what you want to say, before you say it.

If you or anyone else decides to give an impromptu speech, try to keep it short, sweet, and to the point.

Writing Your Own Vows

♥   ♥   ♥   ♥   ♥

In writing your vows, remember that there are no hard-and-fast rules as to what can and cannot be done. Poetry, music, anecdotes about your relationship, religious or famous quotations, and your wishes and dreams for the future can all be incorporated into your declaration of love.

♥

Consult books, Web sites, and wedding magazines that offer samples of vows. Feel free to use portions of these if they appeal to you.

♥

Some couples don't want to write all of their own vows but do want to exchange some personal thoughts during the ceremony. You can use the traditional vows provided by your officiant as the basis for your wedding, but ask him or her to recommend a time during the ceremony when you can exchange your special words.

♥

Practice, practice, practice . . . but not with each other. Have a bridesmaid or your mother give you feedback.

♥

Speaking publicly can be overwhelming—especially if you do not do it often—but if you have prepared in advance, it will be much easier.

♥

Say your vows to one another for the first time at the actual wedding (unless, of course, you have decided to write them together before the ceremony).

♥

Reciting your vows on your wedding day will be more emotional than when you practice before the ceremony, so have tissues on hand.

♥

One couple wrote their vows in the form of letters to each other. For the ceremony, they each assigned to a special friend the honor of reading their letter aloud. One of the groom's friends read the groom's letter to the bride as the groom gazed into his betrothed's eyes, and a female friend read the bride's letter to her groom. This way the couple were free to get choked up without worrying about not being able to finish reading their letters.

♥

Write down your vows and have your maid of honor carry them until it is time for you to read them.

♥

Try not to read the vows right off your cards, and be sure to look into your partner's eyes as much as possible when you say them.

♥

Speak slowly. These words are meaningful and express your promise and commitment to each other from this day forward.

♥

Breathe deeply.

♥

Take your time to savor the passing moment.

♥

Smile.

♥

11

Accessorizing Your Wedding

It is the personal touches that really make a wedding celebration memorable. Your care and attention to detail will be appreciated and noticed by many, so take the time to really think about how you want these elements to be perceived. Accessorize, accessorize, accessorize . . .

Wedding Programs

♥   ♥   ♥   ♥   ♥

Programs can be as simple as a sheet of pretty paper placed on each guest's seat listing the members of the wedding party, those who are doing readings, and short descriptions of traditional elements or facts relating to the ceremony.

•

Consider including a sentence or short phrase after each of the attendants listed, describing their relationship to the bride or groom. This is a nice personal touch and makes guests feel more a part of the ceremony.

•

If you are blending two cultures or religious traditions in your ceremony, include a short description of those traditions in your program so all the guests will feel included and understand the proceedings.

•

Offer a bilingual program (or a translator) if appropriate.

•

You can print your own homemade programs from your computer or copy them at your local printer.

•

Fancy ribbons, sheer papers, and other romantic embellishments can enhance your program if your budget allows or if you so desire.

•

Roll your program up like a scroll, and use a pretty ribbon or a plastic wedding ring to hold it closed.

•

To save money, place one program on every other chair at the ceremony, or have the ushers distribute one per family or couple at the entrance.

•

An "order of events" of the ceremony or a "schedule" of the day or evening festivities can be included to let guests know what the flow of events will be.

•

A personal message from you and your groom to your parents or the guests in general is a nice touch that invitees will enjoy reading while waiting for the ceremony to begin.

•

Programs make nice souvenirs for guests to take home.

•

Programs can also include fun facts about you and your groom, such as the story of your courtship or engagement or your future plans.

•

You can avoid having the same conversation over and over at the reception by putting something about where you'll be honeymooning in the program, too. (Just don't include your contact information!)

•

The back cover can feature a meaningful quotation, poem, or song lyrics that you and your groom choose to share with guests.

•

You can also list what your "something old, something new, something borrowed, something blue" are. These are fun facts for guests to peruse while waiting for the ceremony to begin.

•

One bride and groom even compiled a stapled packet entitled "Wedding Guide of Our Friends and Family— Everything You Wanted to Know about Our Friends and Family but Were Afraid to Ask," and put one in each guest's hotel room. This extensive program included a detailed paragraph on each individual guest, couple, or family and their background and relationship to the bride or groom. If guests were part of the wedding party, their roles were also acknowledged. This program served as an incredible tribute to their friends and family as well as a great way for the guests to get to know one another. It really made the guests feel that the weekend was for them as well as for the bride and groom.

•

Flowers and Decorations

♥   ♥   ♥   ♥   ♥

Choosing a Florist

Shop around. Price ranges and packages will vary greatly, and you may be pleasantly surprised to find that smaller vendors are more flexible in their prices.

When choosing a florist, read the fine print of the contracts and ask lots of questions. They are the experts and can often suggest cost savings or small touches that you may not have considered.

Look at many photo albums of the florists' work in addition to viewing some of their live arrangements.

When you have narrowed your choice to a few florists, have them give you the dates and locations of their current scheduled events where you can take a peek at their live work.

Ask for reference letters or thank you notes the florist has received from previous clients. Call the customers and speak directly with the person who worked with the florist—usually the bride or the mother of the bride—about their thoughts on the experience.

The Bridal Bouquet and Boutonnieres

If your bridal bouquet includes fresh-cut flowers, be sure to wrap the ends in ribbon or fit them with a small water tube so the flower stems do not drip or leak fluid onto yours or the attendants' dresses.

♥

Some brides choose to mix fresh and preserved flowers in their bouquets to save on costs.

♥

If you are carrying silk or dried flowers, be sure to have a sachet of potpourri attached to the handle of the bouquet, or use a scented spray to enhance the bouquet's aroma.

♥

Some brides request that the florist include pot-pourri or floral perfume in all of the bouquets, to en-sure that the air smells nice as the processional occurs.

♥

An ancient custom is to include ivy in the bridal bou-quet, which can later be planted in the couple's garden as a living reminder of the wedding celebration.

♥

Some brides add two white roses to their bouquet. As the bride and her mother walk down the aisle, the bride gives one of the roses to her mother. At the reces-sional, after the couple is officially husband and wife, the bride gives the other rose to her mother-in-law (her new mother).

♥

Some brides choose to carry one simple calla lily tied in a beautiful ribbon as the bouquet, or they use this idea for the bridesmaids' bouquets. It is classy and cost effective.

♥

Hand-tied bouquets are becoming popular for the wedding party. They cost less than the traditional florist's bouquets that are inserted in plastic holders, and they look as though they were freshly picked for the ceremony.

♥

If you can afford it, have two bridal bouquets made instead of one. Use one in all of the pictures and to carry throughout the evening, and use a fresh one for the actual ceremony. That way brown edges and droopy flowers will not be a concern.

♥

When you do the bouquet toss, use one of the brides-maid bouquets so you can save and dry your bridal bouquet as a souvenir.

♥

Don't forget to discuss boutonnieres for the groom, groomsmen, and fathers of the bride and groom; corsages or small arrangements for mothers; and the bridesmaids' bouquets.

♥

Boutonnieres should complement the bridal bouquet.

♥

If you have a going-away outfit, order a corsage to wear on your wrist or to pin on your outfit that coordinates with your bouquet. You can also order a special arrangement of fresh flowers to clip in your hair.

♥

Be sure to bring your bridal bouquet with you to the airport if you are flying somewhere for your honeymoon. The bouquet alone can assist in getting you upgrades or at least complimentary champagne on the flight.

♥

Centerpieces

So that you will not be surprised or disappointed, keep in mind that the arrangements your florist creates for your wedding can sometimes end up being quite different from the vision you discussed with him or her. Arranging flowers is an art form that involves personal interpretation.

•

Keep your centerpieces either low or very high so that your guests will be able to talk to one another during dinner. There is nothing worse than trying to communicate around an obstruction, as beautiful as it may be.

•

Once you have selected your florist, have him or her make up a sample of the centerpiece you have selected so you can see if it is exactly what you want and, if not, so that you can modify it.

•

Potted topiaries—climbing ivy designed around mesh frames in specific shapes—are a fun alternative to floral centerpieces. A ribbon or a few attached flower buds or simple gardenias can make them spiffy.

•

Flowers and candles floating in a fishbowl or a clear glass vase are also simple yet pretty ways to decorate your table.

•

A single flower or a cluster of tiny flowers can be floated in a bowl of water as a simple yet stunning centerpiece. Remember, sometimes less is more.

•

Add a drop of food coloring to clear vases or bowls for a color-coordinated effect that complements your wedding scheme.

•

You could give one randomly chosen guest from each table the privilege of taking home a centerpiece. Perhaps you could put a sticker or a special mark underneath one chair at each table and announce that the person in that seat gets to take home the arrangement.

•

If a person who wins a centerpiece is traveling by plane and cannot preserve or transport it easily, announce that the first person seated to their left who can enjoy it shall be the new winner.

•

After the wedding, donate your centerpieces to a hospital, retirement home, or other deserving charity. Arrange in advance to have someone from the organization pick up the centerpieces after the wedding.

•

Other Tips

Flowers can represent certain traits, characteristics, and meanings. For example, a white rose symbolizes purity and a gardenia means joy. Consult with your florist or read some books on flowers if you would like to have any of your arrangements be symbolic in nature.

Have your florist provide extra flower buds and petals from your arrangements to the cake designer so that he or she can use them on the tiers of your wedding cake or to decorate the cake table.

Use ivy, ribbons, or simple greenery to enhance the ends of church pews or to separate the chairs from the wedding aisle.

Decorate the chairs of the bride and groom with green garlands or fresh flowers and ribbon to set them apart from the rest of the guests.

If you're on a budget, note that fresh flowers will add greatly to the cost of pew or aisle decorations unless you can find a way to reuse them at the reception—for instance, to decorate the wedding cake table or the bride and groom's chairs. Consult chapter 9 for more ways to save money on flowers.

Consider renting topiary trees, hedges, or other greenery to help hide unsightly areas of the reception hall or to accent areas that you want people to focus on. Tiny white twinkling lights or gardenias can be attached to the bushes for a softer effect.

Tall candelabras with their bases garnished in greenery, or with vines and flowers climbing up the base, offer a dramatic effect and save on the cost of flowers.

When using candles, be sure your wedding site regulates the air conditioning properly, so that guests will not be showered in hot wax drippings.

If your wedding ceremony or reception occurs near a pond, pool, or fountain, consider floating flowers and candles in the water. The effect will be dazzling and romantic.

Be careful about using candles at outdoor weddings unless they have a hurricane glass protector around them to prevent them from continually extinguishing throughout the night.

Doing Your Own Flowers or Centerpieces

Be aware that doing your own flowers is more time consuming and time sensitive than you may realize. Do you really want to be worrying about flower quality, quantity, and refrigeration during the few final days before your wedding?

♥

If you do decide to be your own florist, your best bet may be potted plants, bowls with a few floating votives or flowers in them, or silk arrangements.

♥

Consider ordering flowers through your local grocer or home-goods wholesale supplier. You may be pleasantly surprised by their prices and quality.

♥

See if you know anyone who has access to a flower mart or a wholesale flower exchange.

♥

One bride used Disneyland snow globes as her centerpieces surrounded by Disney characters and small flower vases.

♥

Making Signs

♥   ♥   ♥   ♥   ♥

At the entrance of your reception hall or other dining area, hang a large sign welcoming guests to the bride and groom's reception. Perhaps you could print, "Welcome to the reception of Mr. and Mrs. X" to officially use the couple's new name for the first time. A sign of this nature is especially helpful if you are married in a hotel with many different reception rooms. It assists the guests in identifying where to go and adds a more personal touch than the hotel's standard placards.

●

You may choose to have a child decorate your sign with crayons or markers. Or, consider having photos, hearts, or flowers adorn it.

●

Your welcome sign can be as simple as a computerized banner or as extravagant as tulle fabric imbedded with your message and tiny twinkling white lights.

●

Use your welcome sign as a keepsake to hang in your garage someday.

●

Creative Wedding Favors

♥   ♥   ♥   ♥   ♥

Don't feel that you need to provide a favor for every attendee. Couples can take home one favor for the two of them. Singles should receive their own, though.

Tiny silver or ceramic picture frames that also serve as place cards are fun mementos.

Small packets of flower seeds with a message attached, or tiny potted plants that can double as part of the centerpiece or as greenery on the tables, are nice living reminders of your event.

Little glass vases are very inexpensive and can be ordered through florists or craft stores in bulk. Consider attaching place cards to their necks with ribbon and using them to hold part of your tables' floral arrangements. Then add one or two flower cuttings and invite guests to take them home.

Tiny bottles of bubbles printed with your names and wedding date are fun favors. Guests can blow them as you exit the reception and head off to your wedding night.

Golf tees printed with your names and wedding date are a clever idea.

Some couples choose to take the money they would have spent on favors and donate it to a favorite charity. The guests receive a certificate at their place setting describing this choice by the couple, or the donation is announced to guests, so they are aware of the part they played in this philanthropic contribution.

＊

If you are a plant or animal lover, you can place small origami flowers or animals (or plastic figures) on the tables along with a description of the donation that has been made to your favorite charity.

＊

Making your own wedding favors saves money and is also a nice personal touch you can add to your wedding.

＊

Instead of the standard Jordan almonds wrapped in tulle, try other homemade goodies such as fudge, chocolates, brownie squares, or dainty cookies.

＊

One bride and groom ordered two connected white chocolate hearts and had their names written on them in frosting. You could either order a sweet treat like this or make them on your own.

＊

A guest with an instant camera can go from table to table or onto the dance floor to take photos of guests that they can take home that evening as souvenirs. Have preprinted labels with your names and wedding date that can be stuck along the bottom of the photo to make the photos a fun keepsake for guests' refrigerators or photo albums.

Chocolate bars or other wrapped candies with personalized labels are popular favors or dessert treats to have on your tables. Consult wedding magazines, directories, wedding expos, and Web sites that advertise companies that specialize in these types of tasty personal favors.

Some companies make fortune cookies with personalized messages inside. You could have your names and wedding date, or a few special wishes of good fortune personalized for your guests. These cookies are fun to nibble on at dessert and read aloud at the tables.

Insert trivia questions about the bride and groom in fortune cookies for table members to try to answer as a fun party game.

Chocolate-dip personalized fortune cookies and wrap in cellophane for guests to bring home to indulge in later, too.

For an inexpensive but nonetheless special favor, print a meaningful quote, poem, or message to your guests on pretty paper that you can roll up like a scroll and hand-tie for them to take home as a souvenir. (For more money-saving ideas, see chapter 9.)

Matchbooks don't just contain matches anymore. Some have tiny sheets of white paper inside that serve as a little notepad. Have these or regular matchbooks printed with your names and wedding date if this suits your style.

One bride placed LEGO block kits on each table so guests could work together to assemble a creation. These completed projects were then brought to the head table for the bride and groom to save as silly souvenirs. Or try giving mini-LEGO kits as fun favors.

For holiday weddings, incorporate the theme of the holiday into your favor. (For more on holiday or theme weddings, see chapter 8.) For example, a Christmas wedding could give engraved ornaments as favors; a Halloween wedding could give personalized candies; and a New Year's Eve wedding could give personalized candles dated with the New Year.

For table number assignments, one bride used Disney photo magnets with each guest's name and table number inserted. Guests later took these magnets home as favors and souvenirs of the theme wedding.

12 ♥♥♥

Dressing the Bride and Groom

Ahh, the bride in her gown—a vision in white, the princess of the ball. Today is your day to have all eyes on you and to look your best. And as far as the handsome groom, he too will attract the eyes of all, so this is the time to be sure the happy couple looks terrific together.

Dressing the Bride

♥ ♥ ♥ ♥ ♥

The Bride's Vision

Try to have an idea in your mind of the dress you are looking for. That way you will have narrowed down some possibilities before heading to the stores. Doing some homework in advance may make things a bit easier.

•

When you go to the bridal salon, retailer, or dress-maker, bring with you any photos, clippings, or other ideas you have.

•

Consult wedding magazines, photographers' wedding albums, bridal salons and warehouses, and even the Internet for ideas.

•

Make sure your dress reflects the environment in which you are going to be married. For example, if you are having a Catholic wedding in a sacred church, don't wear an off-the-shoulder or revealing dress. On the other hand, for a beachside wedding, less can indeed be more. Even going barefoot is acceptable on the beach!

•

Price-shop and compare.

•

New Trends in Dresses

White is not the exclusive color for brides anymore. Brides wear cream, pastels, or even suits to their weddings.

If you do wear white, you don't have to be the only one. Wedding party attendants can also wear white, which creates a beautiful effect in photos.

For fun, have your "something blue" sewn into your dress, such as a tiny blue flower or a heart that you reveal only to your groom.

Many brides don't want to wear their dress only once, so they buy one that can later be shortened, altered, or even dyed a different color.

Wedding Retailers

If you purchase your gown from a retailer, order it at least six months prior to your wedding date to allow for errors in size, style, or shipping.

♥

Alterations can be time consuming and, during peak wedding seasons, difficult to schedule. Be sure you understand the policies and alteration schedule of your gown maker or distributor before committing to buying your dress from them.

♥

Read all of the fine print in your dress contract—especially regarding your deposit, arrival dates, alteration policies, and damage to the dress. Get everything in writing.

♥

Inquire about return policies or deposit refunds in case your wedding is delayed or, heaven forbid, canceled altogether. You never know, and it is best to be prepared.

♥

Helpful Hints

Practice sitting, dancing, and even kneeling in your dress (if your ceremony requires that). Be sure you can breathe comfortably in every position.

•

A corset or bra with a bustier can shave off inches and hold you into your dress better than you might think. Try one on for size!

•

If your gown has a long train, be sure you practice bustling it with your maid of honor or mother so that there are no complications at the wedding.

•

If your dress is floor length, see about having a band of additional fabric or ribbon banding added to the hem of your wedding dress that can be removed after the wedding is over. The bottom of your dress may be quite dirty after the wedding, and this area is often hard for cleaners or dress preservers to get fully white again.

•

Be old-fashioned and surprise your groom at the wedding with his first view of you in your wedding gown. It makes for an even more dramatic entrance.

•

Half of today's brides change into a going-away outfit before leaving the reception, while the others remain in their wedding dress. Decide what works for you; if budget is an issue, skip the going-away outfit.

•

Fittings and Alterations

Do not schedule your dress fittings to occur after big meals. Granted, you will probably lose weight during the busy final days before the wedding, which your seamstress will account for, but don't make things more difficult on yourself by coming to a fitting with a bloated belly.

Some brides arrive at their final fittings pregnant. If this happens to you, be open and honest with the alterations person so he or she can do what's needed to ensure that you will be comfortable on your wedding day, and can accommodate for any growth in the final weeks before your ceremony.

When getting dressed, cover your face with a light cotton pillowcase or netting before putting the dress over your head to avoid getting makeup on it.

Better yet, if you can step into your gown from the top, you'll prevent makeup smudges and hair messing.

Cleaning and Preserving Your Dress

Wait until after the honeymoon to deal with cleaning your dress. Certain food and beverage stains won't appear on the dress until a few weeks have gone by, and you want to be certain that the cleaner is able to identify and treat all of the stains.

♥

If you wish, you can have your gown preserved after the wedding and sealed in a box for your future daughter or younger relative to wear.

♥

If you decide to preserve your dress, be sure to use a reputable service. Since you can see only a small portion of your dress through the small window in its box, scams have been known to happen. Brides have sadly discovered years later that the dress they paid top dollar to preserve was not in the box.

♥

Bridal Accessories

If you prefer not to wear a veil, consider wearing a wreath of fresh flowers or clipping a few flowers in your hair.

●

Some brides have a two-piece veil: the ceremony veil, which is as long as the train and is removed right before the reception, revealing a shorter veil that is worn for the duration of that event. A hair comb with two strips of Velcro works wonders in securing the two tiers.

●

Some brides have dresses with skirts that can be removed, converting them into a shorter dress that allows more freedom of movement and comfort at the reception. If your dress converts in this way, practice attaching and reattaching the skirt portion a few times before your wedding day.

•

If your dress requires a buttonhook tool or other gadgets to help you put it on, make sure your attendants or mother—whoever will be assisting you on your wedding day—knows how to use them.

•

If you choose to wear gloves during the ceremony, be sure you can slip them off easily when it comes time to put the ring on your finger.

•

On Your Feet

Wear your shoes before the ceremony, and scrape up the bottoms so you don't take a spill down the aisle.

Practice dancing to your wedding song in your shoes so you get used to moving in them.

Be sure to buy shoes one size bigger than normal, even if you have to put shoe pads in them. Your feet will swell during the ceremony and reception, and the extra room will help.

White ballet slippers also work well for wedding-day comfort and look feminine, too.

For extra comfort and practicality, some brides today wear sneakers decorated with pearls, sequins, and lace. If you choose to do so, plan to have a pair of dressier shoes too for your photos, first dance, and other times when your feet may be more visible.

Makeup and Hair

Be sure that your makeup is not too overdone or artificial looking.

♥

Practice putting on your wedding makeup before the big day. Try out the products you'll be using prior to your wedding. No one wants any unexpected allergic reactions or rashes on the big day.

♥

Consult with your photographer to be sure that your makeup will work well with the various environments and types of lighting under which you'll be photographed.

♥

Don't get too suntanned before the wedding. Tan lines look awful in photographs, and in color photographs a too-tanned bride winds up looking orange against the whiteness of her dress.

♥

Advise bridesmaids to not get too suntanned prior to the wedding either, or else they will draw attention away from you and your groom during the ceremony and in photographs.

♥

Have your makeup done by a professional if you can afford it, and coordinate your makeup colors with your wedding party. Perhaps you can all wear the same lipstick color, for example.

♥

Go to a department store makeup counter and have a few of the consultants make you up on various days. If you find someone you like, offer them a job moonlighting for your wedding.

♥

Be sure your foundation or concealer is blended well beneath your eyes and down your neck. You don't want your face to be one color and your neck and arms another.

♥

Ask your photographer about how to use powder to eliminate the glare from flashbulbs on your face. Have your maid of honor keep a compact and tissues on hand to remove perspiration.

♥

Have touch-up makeup in your Bride's Survival Kit (see chapter 1) or a small handbag that your maid of honor can keep track of for you.

♥

Stash an extra lipstick in the ladies' room prior to your ceremony so you can always head there in case of emergency.

♥

Have your makeup and hair done naturally in a way that looks like the real you. If an updo is something you would never wear otherwise, then by all means don't experiment with this look for the first time at your wedding.

♥

Just being the bride will attract plenty of attention to you; you don't need to change your look to do so. You don't want to look back at your pictures after the fact and not recognize yourself because of a dramatic hairdo or excessive makeup.

♥

If the groom is wearing hair gel or having his hair spiffed up in any way, have your maid of honor check him out before the wedding (or take a peek through a crack in the door) to be sure he still looks like himself.

♥

Dressing the Groom

♥   ♥   ♥   ♥   ♥

If the groom's tuxedo has a bow tie, the pre-tied versions are highly recommended. Grooms have been known to look less than smart at their wedding and in photos because they weren't able to tie the bow properly.

●

Be sure that his wedding shoes—whether rented or owned—are comfortable enough to get him through a long day or night.

●

If the shoes are brand new, be sure the bottoms are scraped before the ceremony begins so he doesn't slip.

•

Have the groom's shoes polished before the wedding, and be sure he has appropriate socks to go with his pant and shoe color.

•

The groom should practice wearing any studs, cuff links, and cummerbunds prior to the actual wedding day, and at least once after the final fitting, to be sure that he has all of the loops and hooks figured out.

•

Label the groom's attire. If the male members of the wedding party are all dressed in the same clothing (for instance, tuxes or rented suits), be sure the groom's clothing does not get mixed up in the shuffle.

•

13 ♥♥♥

Hiring the Help

If selecting your wedding party is like choosing players for your team, think of hiring the help as putting together your coaching staff. You want the people you hire to work for you behind the scenes to have your best interests in mind and to know how to pull off a winning wedding. They should have experience, offer good advice, and also know when to pull back. When you find the right people, you'll know it, and the ideas below will help make the process less overwhelming.

The Wedding Coordinator

♥   ♥   ♥   ♥   ♥

Hiring the Coordinator

Be sure that your coordinator is a member in good standing of the Association of Bridal Coordinators (ABC).

•

Contact your coordinator's references, including several brides who have worked with him or her, to make sure the coordinator performed well on those brides' big day.

•

The wedding coordinator can be your best friend or your worst enemy. Before you decide to hire a specific coordinator, be sure that you all get along very well and that he or she is responsive to your needs.

•

Give your coordinator a complete list of the names and numbers of all of your wedding support staff, parents of the bride and groom, wedding attendants, and so on.

•

Discuss your coordinator's attire for the wedding day.

•

What a Coordinator Can Do for You

Defer to your coordinator if he or she has suggestions for florists, bands, caterers, or other wedding support that you may need. Chances are that your coordinator has an amazing network of professionals and services from which to choose, at various price ranges.

Trust that your coordinator will not lead you astray with unnecessary staffing recommendations (even if earning a referral fee!), because he or she wants your event to go as smoothly and seamlessly as possible.

Many brides and grooms feel that a coordinator can be an excellent go-between with their families, especially when divorce or stepparents are involved. Coordinators have had lots of experience in handling sticky family situations and can often be a much-needed (and worth the cost!) ally on the wedding planning front.

The coordinator should be formally introduced to your wedding party as the point person for questions, concerns, or issues that arise on or around the wedding day.

Have your coordinator provide you with a copy of the schedule of wedding day events, from the moment you wake up until you and your new husband drive off together.

Be sure your coordinator also provides schedules to all wedding party members so they know when to be where during the course of the wedding day.

Have your wedding coordinator carry a cell phone and distribute the number so that guests, attendants, and you can reach him or her in case of an emergency.

Assign your coordinator the responsibility for providing special coverage of the men's dressing and preparation area, to make sure that they are running on time, prepared for their photographs, and ready to walk down the aisle.

The Officiant

♥   ♥   ♥   ♥   ♥

Selecting Your Officiant

Choose an officiant who will set the tone you are looking for in your ceremony. See if the officiant has a video of weddings at which he or she has presided, or ask if you can attend an event to see your officiant's style prior to your wedding.

♥

You may want to ask for a copy of the officiant's script before the ceremony to be sure you are comfortable with any references it may contain to your commitment and God or other religious ideas.

♥

Look into your officiant's background, references, or credentials before making a hiring decision. Make sure the officiant is authorized to perform marriages in your state.

♥

Find out if the officiant will attend your wedding rehearsal.

♥

A justice of the peace, judge, or close friend can also do the honors of marrying you if you so choose. (For more on nontraditional officiants, see chapter 6.)

♥

Most of all, be sure you click with your officiant. He or she will be the unifier of you and your fiancé, joining you together in a sacred bond.

♥

Religious Issues

A priest, rabbi, or other religious leader may be your only choice as officiant for church-related and family reasons. Just be sure, when you meet, to communicate what you want and ask lots of questions.

●

If you or your fiancé does not know or has not grown up with the officiant as a religious advisor, be sure that person is comfortable with him or her.

●

The more information you provide about your backgrounds, the history of your relationship, and your life's dreams and aspirations, the more personal your officiant will be able to make your ceremony.

●

If you have an interfaith or intercultural ceremony—one with a priest and a rabbi, for example—be sure that they both contribute equally to the ceremony and that one is not more demonstrative than the other.

●

Some issues with regard to your religious beliefs may be sticky, so be clear and up front with your officiant regarding how you want the religious aspects of your ceremony to be handled.

●

Sometimes a religious leader or judge who is also a close family friend is asked to conduct your ceremony. Often they will refuse to charge you a fee, or the subject of payment will be awkward to discuss. Be sure to give them a personal gift, write a special thank you note, and perhaps donate to their house of worship or other meaningful charity in their name in lieu of monetary compensation.

●

Wedding Documentation and Logistics

Discuss with your officiant any documentation or licenses that you may need prior to or at the actual ceremony. Find out who obtains them or if they are included with the officiant's fee.

Call your local marriage bureau or marital governing organization to inquire about blood tests, required paperwork or other documentation, and fees you will need to pay in order to have your license and marriage recognized by your state.

Inquire about any rules or restrictions on video, audio, or photography equipment at your wedding site.

If you are getting married outdoors, ask whether the officiant will provide audio amplification or whether you should consult with your videographer about that.

Ceremony Specifics

Ask the officiant how he or she feels about the two of you exchanging your own vows, if that is what you would like to do. Some officiants are more strict than others about altering their traditional ceremony script.

♥

If you must turn your back to your guests during the ceremony, be sure that at some point the officiant has you two turn around to look at your guests. The effect is very personal and dramatic.

♥

Try to remember not to look just at the officiant during the ceremony. Look into each other's eyes. After all, you are marrying each other, not your officiant.

♥

If you have children from a previous marriage, ask your officiant how he or she plans to incorporate them into the ceremony. Discuss what you would like and how your officiant has handled this situation in the past.

♥

The Photographer

♥ ♥ ♥ ♥ ♥

Hiring a Professional Photographer

Ask what type of insurance coverage your photographer has for lost or damaged photos.

•

Check his or her references.

•

Be sure to view current samples of a photographer's work before making a hiring decision.

•

Negotiate an agreement that the proofs will be included in the cost of your photo package. These pictures are great to send with thank you notes or to make up mini-albums for grandmothers or special relatives.

•

Also, having the proofs will eliminate the need to order extra individual photos for some family members who request them. You can give them a framed proof instead.

•

Be sure your photographer is sensitive to the details—how your gown is hanging, your hair, if your face is shiny from excitement, and so on—so that he or she can address these issues before taking formal pictures.

•

Ask your photographer to bring two working cameras to your wedding, just in case one of them malfunctions or the film is bad.

•

Have your photographer and videographer film the moment when your groom first sees you, whether it is before your session with the photographer or at the moment the doors open and you begin walking down the aisle. This candid image of his facial expression is worth a thousand words.

•

Make a master list for your photographer of all the formal shots you want taken, detailing the particular groupings you would like so you are sure to get at least one picture that includes each of your most important guests.

•

Get everything in writing and read all of the fine print in your contracts. Be sure you understand all of the points of your contract, including issues of deposit refunds and loss or damage to pictures, before signing on any dotted lines.

•

Other Photography Options

Assign your photographer's assistant, or a guest whose hobby is photography (and wouldn't mind), to take only candid pictures. That way you ensure that some of the spontaneous moments are caught on film.

✳

Some high-tech photographers offer, for an added cost, to have their assistant take pictures with a digital camera. By doing this, they can actually produce a mini–photo album by the end of your wedding for you and your guests to see instantly.

✳

Plus, with digital photos, the bride and groom don't have to wait until after the honeymoon or until wedding proofs arrive to see images of the event.

✳

As a gift to the bride and groom, one guest obtained a guest list and took a picture of everyone in attendance, using an instant camera. Some pictures were taken in groups and others alone. She inserted these into an album and had the guests jot a note at the base of the photo or on the album page as a kind of photographic sign-in book. By the end of the wedding, the book was completed and she presented it to the bride and groom. The cost of the film and album came out to about what she had planned to spend on their gift, and this was an instant souvenir that they could cherish forever.

✳

✳

On the Wedding Day

See for yourself that your photographer has film in his or her camera and that the used rolls are being put in a safe place. Unfortunately, mistakes have been known to happen!

♥

If you have a theme wedding where guests come dressed in costume or other attire related to your theme, consider hiring an additional photographer to take portraits of these guests in a designated area with a fun backdrop. The photos can then be given or mailed to them as wedding favors.

♥

Consider having black-and-white photos taken during your wedding. The effect is timeless.

♥

Know that color photos can be reprinted in black and white if you so desire. Black-and-white film cannot, however, be converted to color; it can only be hand-tinted.

♥

The Videographer

♥ ♥ ♥ ♥ ♥

Hiring the Videographer

Get everything in writing and read all of the fine print in your contracts. Be sure you understand all of the points of your contract, including issues of deposit refunds and loss or damage to videotape, before signing on any dotted lines.

•

Be sure to view current samples of a videographer's work before making a hiring decision.

•

Check his or her references.

•

Reach an agreement with the videographer about how many guest interviews you want included in your tape. If the videographer will not be bringing an assistant, you don't want him or her tied up interviewing guests while other events are happening that should be recorded.

•

Ask to review the raw footage of your video prior to the final edits so that you can choose to eliminate any extraneous elements that you don't feel compelled to include, such as extra-long toasts or too much footage of the dance floor.

•

Video Details

Choose songs for your videographer to incorporate that pertain to your relationship. There is nothing worse than watching the precious moments of your wedding day set to elevator music or other songs that do not appeal to you.

Give the videographer CDs or cassette tapes labeled with a list of the songs you would like as background music, as well as a master list of these songs, so that you can be sure the video will use the music you enjoy.

✳

A montage of photos of you and your spouse at different stages in life as you grew up makes for a fun opening to your video. Be sure to follow this with highlights of your relationship leading up to the wedding.

✳

Watch your wedding video and look through your photo album on every anniversary to remind yourself and your spouse of the joy you experienced on that day.

✳

Photographer and Videographer Duties

Arrange with both your videographer and photographer to have two cameras going during the procession and ceremony. That way you'll have images of the wedding party as they enter and exit as well as the bride and groom's faces and reactions throughout.

♥

Put your videographer and photographer in contact before the wedding so they can make sure that their various supplemental lighting and equipment will not conflict with each other's work.

♥

✳

Be sure the videographer places a three- to five-minute recap of the entire wedding at the end of your video, so in the future you can show just that portion to friends and family who may not have the patience to sit through your whole wedding tape(s).

♥

The Musicians

♥   ♥   ♥   ♥   ♥

Hiring the Musicians

DJs will typically be a less expensive option than a live band. Decide with your partner how important this element of your wedding is to you and what your budget limitations are.

•

Arrange a time to hear your prospective DJ or band at a live event prior to hiring them or, at a minimum, prior to your wedding so that you can offer feedback or comments as to your desires and expectations.

•

Check the references of your band or DJ from multiple sources: brides and grooms who have used them, wedding coordinators or hotels that have worked with them, and so on.

•

Read the DJ or band's contract closely with regard to their policy on overtime payments as well as any hidden costs you may incur such as setup and take-down fees, permit fees, meal costs, frequency of breaks, or insurance.

•

Ask a lot of questions.

●

Choose your song list in advance of the wedding to ensure that you and your guests enjoy the selections.

●

If your band or DJ does not offer certain songs that are important to you, see if they will learn or locate them. At least offer your own personal copies for their use at the event.

●

Check what music selections will be played during the musicians' breaks to be sure you like what they have chosen. You don't want to eat dinner to classical music if you would prefer soft jazz.

●

Some weddings use DJs that provide interactive entertainment such as teaching guests the bunny hop, samba, Electric Slide, or Macarena. Be sure you discuss these choices with your DJ prior to the wedding so there are no surprises and so you do not feel that they are overinvolved in the flow of things.

●

Some DJs or bands bring maracas, costume paraphernalia, and even backup dancers to mingle with the guests on the dance floor. Be sure you agree to and desire these added elements at your wedding.

●

You and the groom, not the musical performers, are the stars of the evening . . . unless, of course, you want them to be. Make your wishes clear up front.

●

The First Dance

Before the wedding, take dancing lessons together so you'll look good during your all-important first dance. The classes are fun and will get you motivated for the big day.

If you don't want to spring for more expensive dance lessons, check with your local college or community center's dance program. See if the instructor will moonlight and give you a few private lessons to help you choreograph your first dance, or at least teach you a few moves that you two can practice and feel comfortable doing together. You will probably find these private lessons to be cheaper than formal group dance classes.

One American groom and his Argentinean bride learned to tango together for their first dance. The bride even changed into a red dress with fishnet stockings and the groom actually held a rose between his teeth. It was great entertainment, and the bride and groom had a ball as they displayed the wonderful blending of their cultural heritages.

Warning: If you choose a song for your first dance that is currently on the pop music charts, you may not be able to ask a band to play "your song" on future anniversaries because they won't know it. At a minimum, have a timeless tune as your secondary wedding song so that you'll be able to dance to it on anniversaries well into the future without digging up your old CD or tape.

If you want to have the wedding party join you on the dance floor during the first dance, make sure you and your fiancé have some time alone on the dance floor first, before the band or DJ calls up the rest of the party, so that guests can enjoy watching the two of you dance as husband and wife.

Choose a special song for the father-daughter dance and invite your groom to do a mother-son dance if he so desires.

The Hora

If you do the hora for a Jewish wedding, be sure you enlist strong men to lift the chairs that you and your groom will be sitting atop.

♥

Have the best man or groom explain the significance of this festive dance prior to the ceremony so that the designated men know what to expect with regard to their weightlifting duties.

♥

You may also want to have young uncles, cousins, or close friends who are not a part of the wedding party on stand-by to assist with the lifting.

♥

Be sure to use chairs with arms for the hora since brides and grooms have been known to fall or get knocked off during the excitement of it all. Armchairs give them a better grip to hang on tight.

♥

Reception Dancing and Music

If you are having a Mardi Gras or New Year's Eve theme wedding, audience participation dances may be more appropriate than at a formal sit-down affair.

•

Be sure to select a few songs that appeal to every generation attending so that all guests will feel included and inspired to get up and dance.

•

Have your wedding coordinator, groom, or best man be the middleman between you and the band if you have any comments you'd like to make during the reception. The bride shouldn't need to be going up to the stage to chat with them.

•

If you are unhappy with some of the band's antics, their volume, or their level of involvement with the guests (too much or too little), communicate that to them via your middleman throughout the course of the night.

•

The same goes for your pleasure with their performance. If you praise them, they will continue to work hard.

•

Some computer-savvy couples of the new millennium are using an MP3 player at their weddings, which can organize preselected songs via a computer and play them at the reception or during the dance portion of your celebration.

•

If you and your fiancé are the more daring sort, seek out a singing celebrity impersonator to add some fun and humor to your wedding reception. If you two are big Elvis, Frank Sinatra, or Barbra Streisand fans, your city should have someone who can liven up the party.

•

Personal Touches

If you or your fiancé are musically inclined, consider writing a song for each other to use as your wedding song or just to sing at the reception.

If someone from your wedding party or a close friend will be singing during your ceremony or at the reception, discuss this in advance with your band or DJ. Put your singer in touch with the musicians prior to the wedding so they can discuss key details of accompaniment.

If both your and your fiancé's parents are still married (or if just one set is married and this would not be awkward), arrange to have their wedding song(s) played at some point during the reception. This will please them.

Transportation

♥   ♥   ♥   ♥   ♥

Guest Transportation

Provide guests with detailed directions, the phone numbers of wedding-related locations, and an emergency cell phone contact number to call if they have any problems getting from place to place.

♥

For out-of-town guests or those who do not rent cars, you may want to provide group transportation by buses or minivans.

♥

Arrange for your local friends to transport out-of-town guests to events or between the ceremony site and reception hall (if they are located in different places).

♥

A decorated car or a double-decker bus is a fun way to transport guests around the area for sightseeing or wedding events.

♥

Provide the bus or van drivers with detailed directions for each destination as well as contact phone numbers for the place they are going, in case they get lost or stuck in traffic.

♥

Be sure bus or van drivers are equipped with CB radios or cell phones so they can alert the wedding coordinator or location manager of any delays.

♥

Arrange assistance for elderly guests or those with special needs.

♥

Bride and Groom Transportation

Consider alternatives to the traditional (and expensive) limousine exit. You could go by horse-drawn carriage, boat, hot-air balloon, taxi, streetcar, vintage automobile, motorcycle, convertible, horseback, or even tandem bicycle if your dress permits. Choose a fun and clever send-off if that suits your style or wedding theme.

•

Have a friend be your chauffeur in a rented town car.

•

Arrange for food and beverage to be waiting for you in the limousine or car in which you exit. Chances are you will have eaten very little at the wedding and won't realize how ravenous you are until you get into the car.

•

Be sure to have a few extra slices of wedding cake packed away for you to nibble on at the hotel. Wedding cake tastes great as a midnight snack in your honeymoon suite or for breakfast the morning after!

•

Is someone from your wedding party planning to decorate your going-away car with balloons, a "Just Married" sign, empty cans, or shoes tied to the bumper? These touches make for a more festive send-off.

•

Other fun ways to decorate your exit vehicle include fresh or silk flowers, streamers, painted messages on the windows, pom-poms or ribbons attached to the antenna, and even a funny enlarged photo of the couple displayed in the rear window.

•

Have the driver of your send-off car drive you around through your town or city if you so desire. This is the one time that all eyes are on you, and you may want to relish the moment even more.

•

Kiss, cuddle, and savor your first drive together down the highway of life as husband and wife.

•

14 ♥♥♥

Eat, Drink, and Be Merry

The ceremony is over and the guests are hungry. Full tummies mean happy people, so be sure you have planned for ample food and drink to keep your guests in a celebratory mood. As you will discover below, there are many ways to feed your guests besides the traditional sit-down dinner. As wedding ceremonies have become more unique, the rules regarding appropriate fare have become more flexible, too. Bon appétit!

Feeding the Masses

♥   ♥   ♥   ♥   ♥

Hiring the Caterer

When selecting your wedding site, catering issues will arise. Your options and limitations will vary depending on whether you choose a hotel sit-down reception or a beachside buffet barbecue.

●

For hotel or banquet hall receptions, set up a meeting with the caterer and map out your budgetary constraints, dietary restrictions, dream menu, and other food-related desires.

●

If you are hiring your own caterer, call the references of those you are considering. See if other brides were happy with their experience working with them.

●

Be sure that your caterer is insured and licensed to protect against any unforeseen problems that may arise at the reception.

●

Determine if it is more cost effective for you to have a sit-down meal, a buffet meal, or a heavy hors d'oeuvres and cake reception. The options run the gamut, and you can decide what works best for your group size and budget.

●

Don't accept the first number that a caterer throws out. Negotiate until you are comfortable with the price.

•

Most caterers will offer you tastings of menu items so you can sample the various foods that could be served at your event and determine which food combinations appeal to you. Take advantage of the tastings, and bring your fiancé along!

•

You might especially want to savor the tasting since you may not have time to sit down and enjoy the meal at your actual reception.

•

Check to see if your caterer can get you any price breaks on beverages or your wedding cake.

•

Be sure to ask your caterer what is the final possible date you can submit your head count for guests. Many guests RSVP at the last minute, and you do not want to be penalized or pay for extra meals that go uneaten.

•

Ask to see the china that your food will be served on to make sure that it is not too patterned and won't clash with your centerpieces, table covers, or food presentation.

•

See if your caterer will provide a simple plate of food (perhaps a pared-down version of your wedding meal) for your band, DJ, wedding coordinator, photographer, videographer, and so on if their contracts so specify.

•

Ask your caterer to prepare two extra plates of food and some slices of wedding cake for you and your groom to eat after the wedding, either in the send-off car or in your hotel room. You will be hungry!

•

Menu Ideas

Consider including in your menu a special dish that commemorates your or your groom's heritage.

Be sure your caterer has a few kosher or vegetarian plates prepared on stand-by for any guests that you know have dietary restrictions or allergies.

If you have food choices on your RSVP cards, such as chicken or beef, be sure that your caterer has a system in place to accommodate guests so the servers don't have to ask, "Chicken or beef?" of every guest. Perhaps your table place cards can be discreetly marked to alert servers.

For weddings with a theme such as Hawaii or New Orleans Mardi Gras, incorporate authentic foods from these regions into your menu.

Some brides and grooms choose to place personalized menus on the tables with their names and wedding date followed by a listing of the courses and how they are prepared. This may assist curious guests or those with food allergies and also serves as a nice souvenir of your event.

Hors d'Oeuvres

If you choose to take formal group and wedding party photos after your ceremony, be sure that the guests receive hors d'oeuvres, or offer vegetable and cheese-and-cracker platters so they can nibble while they await your entrance.

♥

The same goes for receiving lines. If you have a receiving line following your ceremony, arrange to have hors d'oeuvres or beverages offered to the guests who are waiting in line.

♥

If hors d'oeuvres are being passed, a nice touch is to have the waiter hold a stack of napkins monogrammed with the bride and groom's first names or new married name and wedding date. You can always use the leftover napkins for future entertaining at your new home.

♥

If a meal is not served at your wedding and you offer only heavy hors d'oeuvres and cocktails (followed by cake or a dessert table, of course!), be sure that guests do not have to stand on their feet for too long. Even if you do not have formal table assignments, be sure there are enough seating areas so guests can visit and relax.

♥

Dining Options

Some receptions offer the guests a variety of foods presented in buffet-style food stations. One station may have prime rib and fresh-cut turkey; another might offer sushi; and a third could be a make-your-own-pasta station.

•

A huge benefit of food stations is that guests can serve themselves, get food while it is hot, and choose what appeals to them instead of being restricted by a preset menu. Plus, guests can return to stations as much as they want to refill their plates.

•

If you have a buffet or food station–style meal, be sure that a head waiter or your caterer personally goes around to each table to invite guests to serve themselves. Otherwise you'll have chaos at the food stations or a buffet line that winds around the block.

•

If you have a buffet reception, be sure that the table attendants keep the guests' glasses full of water, wine, or their beverage of choice, unless you have pitchers on each table or offer a self-serve beverage area.

•

If you choose to have a set menu, consider eliminating the dessert course and having the wedding cake be offered alone. You'll save money, and most people don't eat two desserts anyway.

•

Budget Ideas

Have a brunch wedding, where guests select from a make-your-own-omelet or Belgian waffle station, fruit platters, and a variety of pastries.

✳

Hot tea with small cakes and finger sandwiches is another easy idea for brunch weddings.

✳

Visit a local culinary institute or cooking school to see if any students or chefs there would be interested in catering your reception. The students may cost a great deal less, need the experience, and will probably work even harder if they are given any class credit for catering your event.

✳

Find out if the cost of renting china is included in your meal price or if it is additional.

✳

Be sure you have an accurate total of your costs so you are not surprised with unexpected bills after the event.

✳

Arrange to have leftovers donated to a local soup kitchen or charitable organization after the wedding. Maybe your caterer can arrange to have the food delivered or can help you select that appropriate recipient.

✳

✳

Feeding Children

See if your caterer will offer a children's menu selection if you will have youngsters at your wedding. There is no sense in paying for a fancy four-course meal for a child who will not eat it.

♥

A separate children's table for ages four and up (since smaller ones will probably eat with their parents) is a nice option to offer to your little guests.

♥

If you are having a children's table, entrees of grilled cheese sandwiches, hamburgers, or macaroni and cheese, with French fries on the side, are great, inexpensive choices.

♥

If many children will be attending your reception, a kids' mini-buffet, a small sundae bar, or a milkshake station could be fun additions. Consult with your caterer.

♥

Have some activities at the children's table such as crayons, coloring books, LEGOs or small blocks, or even a simple art project or puzzles to keep them occupied.

♥

Arrange to have nannies or baby sitters to watch the children so their parents can enjoy the adult reception.

♥

Just be sure that the nannies or sitters have a list of the children's names and their parents' table numbers in case they need to locate the adults during the meal.

♥

Beverages: May Their Cup Runneth Over

♥　♥　♥　♥　♥

Classy and Unique Touches

Have a thin lemon slice floating in each water glass or, at a minimum, in the pitchers for a classy, inexpensive touch.

●

On the tables, also offer flavored sparkling water in attractive bottles. Or tie ribbons around the necks of bottles to make them more visually appealing.

●

Consider having a coffee bar or espresso station for guests as a special treat. Be sure your caterer positions a person there to assist guests in preparing coffee drinks or restocking the area.

●

Have a punch bowl where guests can serve themselves. Spiff it up with heart- or flower-shaped ice cubes and even frozen sparkling water. Float some lemon slices in the bowl as well.

●

Serve a vintage of wine at your wedding from the calendar year of your wedding, engagement, or other significant year such as your date of birth.

•

Have a magnum (huge bottle) of champagne for all the guests to share at your champagne toast.

•

Save the bottle as a souvenir and encourage guests to sign or write a message on it with a metallic pen.

•

Don't forget to have a wide selection of nonalcoholic beverages from which to choose.

•

Tiny bottles of wine or champagne, printed with personalized labels bearing your names and wedding date, are a nice party favor to give your guests.

•

Serve fun drinks with miniature umbrellas, floating fruit, or silly straws to liven things up.

•

Have special goblets or crystal glasses monogrammed for you and the groom to use for toasts at your wedding. These will make great keepsakes, too.

•

You can also order a romantic set of silver-plated champagne flutes that fit together in the shape of a heart. Each of you can drink out of one half of the heart. (Many bridal magazines or boutiques sell these items.)

•

Let Them Eat Cake

♥   ♥   ♥   ♥   ♥

Hiring the Baker

Bring your baker clippings, photos, and clear descriptions of the cake you envision.

Some specialty bakers make only a limited number of wedding cakes a week because they are so labor intensive. Book your baker early if this is the case.

Be certain that your reception hall approves of the baker or other outside food contractors that you are using. Sometimes there are insurance issues that you may be unaware of, so clear their names through the location manager before committing to them.

If you personally know a talented chef or baker, see if they will make your cake as a wedding gift to you.

New Cake Trends

White-tiered cake with white frosting is not the only way to go anymore. Modern couples select such flavors as mocha, carrot, zucchini, strawberries and cream, lemon, cheesecake, and almost any flavor you can imagine. Taste many before deciding!

♥

You can also have several different flavors of cake by having one flavor for each tier.

♥

If you have a theme wedding, consider having a cake that reflects your theme. For example, if your wedding has a Hawaiian theme, have your cake shaped like a hula dancer or a palm tree.

♥

Cakes come in all shapes and sizes nowadays. Some are decorated to look like stacks of wrapped presents, while others are shaped like hearts.

♥

Cakes can have an edible photo-like image of the bride and groom across the top, while others can be covered in flakes of freshly grated chocolate.

♥

A groom's cake is typically a small, richly flavored cake displayed alongside the wedding cake. Some couples choose to serve a sliver of this with the wedding cake, or they box up individual slices to be sent home with guests.

♥

If you choose to have a groom's cake, consider a fun, whimsical design. For example, the cake could be shaped like sports paraphernalia, have a funny photo of the groom on top, or represent a hobby the groom pursues. For instance, if he is a fisherman, the cake could be shaped like a trout. Or, if he loves attending basketball games, the cake could shaped like a basketball or designed to look like a ticket to his favorite team's game. Be creative!

♥

Tasty Tips

Use a small one- or two-tier wedding cake to cut and feed each other at the reception, while having sheet cakes of the same flavor in the back, presliced by the caterer and ready to serve.

●

Discuss with your groom prior to the wedding how you plan to handle the sharing of the first bite of cake. Some brides do not like having cake smeared on their faces, but if this suits your styles, then go for it.

●

Save the top tier of your wedding cake to eat at your one-year anniversary. Cover it in plastic wrap and then tin foil. Then place it in a small box and wrap the box in plastic wrap and foil before freezing it. This should both prevent freezer burn and preserve the taste of the cake until your anniversary.

●

Avoid saving cake that is made with fresh fruit, though, as it may not survive the year.

●

Clever and Classy Touches

Consider some fun alternatives to traditional bride and groom cake toppers: Barbie and Ken dolls, action figures, fresh flowers that are coordinated with your bouquet, painted hearts, cupids or doves from your local craft store, Minnie and Mickey Mouse figurines, or even a custom-made bride and groom figures that are crafted out of chocolate or almond paste to actually resemble you and your groom.

Tie French ribbon on your cake knife and around the base of the champagne flutes that will be on the cake table. This makes for an inexpensive yet elegant touch.

Decorate your cake table with a coordinating table-cloth, ribbons, bridesmaids' bouquets, or fresh flowers so it looks attractive for your pictures.

One couple received a cake knife as a wedding gift, which was engraved with their names and wedding date. They used it to cut their cake, and it then became a beautiful memento to use for future entertaining.

Some receptions offer a dessert table or another dessert as well as the cake. If this fits your budget, it is a welcome addition.

15 ♥

Second Weddings

Getting married for the second or third time is almost commonplace in our society. Are there any second-wedding issues you should be concerned about? These ideas for getting married again should help you cruise through the planning stages and enjoy the smooth ride of finding the right person once and for all.

Benefits of Second Weddings

♥　　♥　　♥　　♥　　♥

Second weddings can actually be much more fun and less stressful to plan than first weddings. A second wedding is typically your chance to do anything and everything you wanted to do at your first but couldn't, because of either family issues, budget constraints, or the pressure of tradition. So have fun and go for it!

●

You may be able to save friends and family the hassle and expense of gifts (and yourself the time involved in registering), since you probably already have many of the things you will need as a married couple. This wedding can focus more on your celebration of love and happiness in finding one another.

●

The nicest benefit of a second wedding is that you have more experience, hindsight, and a second chance to have found your soul mate. Congratulations and enjoy the fun!

●

Announcing Your News

♥   ♥   ♥   ♥   ♥

You can do this formally, as you would for a first wedding, by contacting local newspapers, friends, and family and even sending out announcements, or you can be more low-key and simply call those closest to you to share your news.

Consider and be sensitive to the impact that your news may have on your children from previous marriages or on your ex-spouse(s).

Because your second wedding may be significantly different in size or scope than your first, be careful about whom you tell of your news right away. They may assume that they are going to be included in or invited to your ceremony.

✳

Consider announcing your wedding plans at the same time you share your news. For example, if you plan to do a reception only and to include just immediate family (or no one) in your ceremony, it may be good to be up front with your plans when you make your round of calls.

✳

In wording your invitations, there are no rules you must follow. You can be really creative and even handwrite the invitations if that suits your style.

✳

Do not feel obligated to send out a formal, engraved, traditional invitation unless you want to.

✳

Many second weddings are paid for not by the couple's parents but by the bride and groom. If this is the case for you, there is no need to refer to your parents in the invitation unless you choose to do so.

✳

If this is a second wedding for only one of you, some parents may be involved in funding your event. If so, discuss with them the invitation wording or other parental references in your announcements, wedding program, or ceremony.

✳

✳

Lack of Rules

♥   ♥   ♥   ♥   ♥

The biggest rule to remember is that there are no rules or set way to have a second wedding. Second weddings come in all shapes and sizes. Just go with your instincts.

♥

Keep in mind that unforeseen issues may arise that may take a bit more patience and sensitivity than you needed when planning your first wedding. Complications regarding ex-spouses, children from a previous marriage, and even ex–in-laws have been known to emerge.

♥

Keep your sense of humor and focus on what is really important: your love for your newfound partner.

♥

Just as there are no rules to follow in planning second weddings, there are also no rules that govern how guests should react or behave with regard to your news or at your wedding. Expect that some, especially friends from your previous circle that included your ex, may not respond with gifts and heartfelt congratulations. Your new situation may take some getting used to, so perhaps congratulations may not come right away . . . give it time.

♥

In some couples, only one of the two has been married before, which can pose some complications. Many women who marry divorced or widowed men, for instance, still want to have the big wedding. In this case, the groom should indulge his bride. She wants to do this once and do it right, so it's only fair to let her lead the way.

♥

When it's the man who is marrying for the first time and the woman for her second, chances are you may be able to do something other than the large traditional wedding. Destination weddings, a smaller reception, or even eloping to Las Vegas may suit you just fine, and you'll run into fewer hassles and complications. (Consult chapters 7 and 8 for ideas on creative ways to wed.)

♥

Can the bride wear white? Most certainly, if that is what she wishes.

♥

Some second-time brides prefer a simple suit or dress to a traditional wedding gown.

♥

The majority of second-time brides choose not to wear a veil.

♥

If either of you are still close to your ex-spouse(s), consider inviting them to the wedding if this is not too awkward a gesture and will not come as a shock to your fiancé. If you have children, it may make them feel more comfortable about your remarriage, too.

♥

If you do choose to register for gifts, smaller-ticket items would be appropriate. Also, any appliances you have from your first marriage can certainly be updated with newer models. If you are divorced, you probably had to split many of your items with your ex, so you may want to start fresh with some new dishes or appliances.

♥

Even if you register, though, don't be surprised if some guests don't bring you a substantial gift —or any gift, for that matter—especially if they attended your first wedding and gave you a gift then.

♥

In lieu of gifts, request that your guests make a donation to the charity of your choice.

♥

Avoid comparing your second wedding to your first. This can upset your fiancé, and it is better to focus on the current wedding.

♥

Incorporating Children from Previous Marriages

♥   ♥   ♥   ♥   ♥

Be sensitive when including children from previous marriages in your ceremony. While the idea may be a genuine gesture of love and openness, it may make your children feel guilty with respect to their other parent (your ex).

•

Communicate with your children openly to see if their participation would be detrimental to your relationship or difficult for the children to handle. First and foremost, be sensitive to your children's feelings and needs.

•

Children can be given honors such as best man or maid of honor, flower attendant, ring bearer, or some other role to play that will make them feel special.

•

Give your children some other fun wedding duties. One bride put her son in charge of making the sign for the send-off car and decorating the wedding program. Another groom had his daughter give him away, and she walked him down the aisle.

●

Be sure that the duties you bestow upon children are age appropriate. For example, two- and three-year-olds aren't big on walking down aisles alone unless accompanied by a sibling or parent.

●

Give your children a token or gift to show them that you are bringing them into your new marriage with open arms. It's an excellent way to make them feel a part of things.

●

Ideas for children (depending on age) include a small wedding ring, necklace, or other piece of jewelry; a pet; something else they have been wanting for a long time; or an age-appropriate getaway, such as a trip to Disneyland or another theme park with you and your fiancé, to celebrate your impending family union.

●

16

Other Ways to Wed

In the new millennium, there are many ways to wed that a generation ago would have raised many an eyebrow. So don't be afraid to be daring; be true to your convictions, and make your wedding day just what you've always dreamed it would be.

Eloping and Civil Ceremonies

♥   ♥   ♥   ♥   ♥

Eloping (getting married without telling anyone first) appeals to some couples because it avoids financial, religious, or other conflicts or personal issues that may otherwise arise in the course of planning a wedding ceremony.

●

Couples getting married for a second or third time often elope because it cuts down on many potential complications. For example, a wedding ceremony that involves blended families and stepparents might become a family political battle, making elopement more inviting.

●

So if you two feel that eloping is for you, go for it: Get on a plane to Vegas or visit your justice of the peace or courthouse.

●

One long-engaged couple got married on the spur of the moment while on vacation in Hawaii, after discovering that their hotel had a wedding coordinator who could arrange it all for them.

●

Understand that if you do elope, however, some friends and family may be offended, or at least miffed, and may need a bit of time to accept or embrace your situation.

●

Expect that eloping may severely reduce the number of gifts you'll receive. Some people may feel slighted because you did not include them in a ceremony or, at a minimum, a reception.

●

On that note, consider having a reception, no matter how informal, to publicly celebrate and have your union recognized by family and friends. This allows those close to you to offer you their personal congratulations and feel included in your marriage.

•

There is nothing wrong with heading to your local courthouse to say "I do" in a quick, clean, simple ceremony. In some ways, civil ceremonies are very old-fashioned and uniquely romantic.

•

Some couples may want to do a civil ceremony to legalize their commitment, and then plan a more elaborate celebration at a later date.

•

If cost is an issue for you, civil ceremonies and eloping are your best options.

•

Interfaith and Intercultural Marriages

♥   ♥   ♥   ♥   ♥

Weddings that blend two nationalities, languages, religions, or cultures can often be more complex than others.

If you have a formal wedding ceremony, consider using programs to explain your unique traditions or cultural references. (See chapter 11 for more on wedding programs.)

Be sure that your officiant gives "equal time" to both heritages, so that one is not favored over the other.

Better yet, hire two officiants, one representing each religion or culture, to co-conduct your ceremony.

✳

If your marriage blends two different languages, hire a translator for guests or have your officiant conduct a bilingual ceremony.

✳

Despite the fact that those you invite to your wedding are supposedly your dearest and closest family and friends, you may receive some naïve or even insensitive comments from older-generation guests or others who may not readily embrace your union. Let any insensitive remarks fall like water from a duck's back.

✳

Remember the American groom and Argentinean bride mentioned earlier who got married in the United States and decided to acknowledge the bride's heritage by performing Argentina's most traditional dance, the tango, as their first dance at the reception? The guests were dazzled!

✳

Remember that this is *your* wedding. Don't let anyone dictate to you or rain on your parade.

✳

If your wedding blends two cultures or languages, incorporate traditions from both of your heritages into the ceremony.

✳

You may want to have two wedding celebrations, one in each country or region. For instance, one couple had one wedding in the United States for her side of the family and another in Korea for his side of the family.

Parents and some very close friends and family of the couple attended both ceremonies, but the majority of the guest list was different in each country due to travel costs and time limitations.

You may choose to each recite your vows in your individual mother tongue.

Same-Sex Marriages

There are no rules when it comes to commitment or unity ceremonies. You can design your own criteria and tweak and bend those elements that you have witnessed at traditional weddings.

Even if your marriage is not recognized as legal by your state, there is no reason not to pull out all of the stops and have the wedding of your dreams.

Commitment ceremonies can be as elaborate or as simple as you wish. Just be sure that both of you are comfortable with the style of your ceremony.

The guests you choose to invite should appeal to both of you. The guest list can often be sensitive to compile in cases where one partner's family does not happily embrace your union. Just be sure that the people you include in your celebration are truly there to celebrate with and for you.

Anyone can perform your ceremony if there are no legal considerations involved. If you choose to have a judge or a justice of the peace, be sure that this person's ceremony text reflects the vision of your union. (Consult chapter 13 regarding hiring your officiant.)

♥

Check with your local gay or lesbian association for lists of people who perform same-sex ceremonies.

♥

A local bookstore, the library, or the Internet may have information on other local offices of national organizations that may be able to assist in your ceremony plans.

♥

Consider having programs to explain to your guests the components of your ceremony and to list your attendants.

♥

Since there are no traditional legal vows for same-sex marriages, this is your chance to declare your love for each other in your own unique way, in front of those nearest and dearest to you.

♥

Feel free to modify any vows you have heard elsewhere. Consult books, the Internet, poems, songs, and chapter 10 of this book.

♥

Wear your rings on whichever hand you choose. Again, there are no rules as to what is right or wrong. Many same-sex couples wear their rings on the right hand, a symbolic alternative to the traditional practice. Others choose to wear them on the left hand.

♥

In some lesbian weddings, both women wear wedding gowns, while other couples choose to have one partner wear a gown and the other wear a suit or tuxedo. Discuss with your partner what would be right for you two. The same goes for male unity ceremonies.

♥

Your wedding can and should include all of the elements of a traditional wedding, such as a formal reception, dancing, a cake, registering for gifts, and, of course, a honeymoon.

♥

Marrying Later in Life

♥   ♥   ♥   ♥   ♥

Realize that a wedding later in life can be as elaborate or simple as you wish.

●

Your wedding may include grown children and even grandchildren. Just be sure that you embrace all who attend and still preserve what is important to you in defining this special love that you have been blessed with later in your life.

●

Don't feel that because you are older it is not worth getting married to "legalize your union." Couples marrying later in life often share a passion for finding a true companion with whom to share their golden years.

●

Grandchildren and even great-grandchildren could play a special role in your ceremony.

•

Eloping or destination weddings are ideal—make a vacation out of it.

•

17

Renewing Your Vows, or Reaffirmation Ceremonies

Renewing your vows is a true celebration and symbolic reminder of your commitment and continued love for one another. Couples choose to renew for many reasons, among them to celebrate a milestone in their marriage such as a special anniversary, or to jump-start their marriage after some sort of downfall or difficult period. Whatever your reasons, enjoy the high of recommitting yourselves to each other.

Why Renew Your Vows?

♥　　♥　　♥　　♥　　♥

If you two are happily married, why not do it all over again?

•

You can choose a special date for your event: com-memorate an anniversary, the day you first kissed, or even your engagement.

•

Renewing your vows can be symbolic of a new be-ginning or a new chapter in your lives. For example, if your marriage has been rocky or you have been in coun-seling, you may want to renew your love for one an-other and get a fresh start.

•

If you have overcome a serious crisis, perhaps you have reason to celebrate your love.

•

You can also re-propose with a ring, necklace, or other token of love to symbolize your re-union.

•

A vow renewal ceremony is a chance to have the wed-ding you never had. Maybe you eloped or did not have enough money for the wedding of your dreams. Renew-ing your vows later in your marriage can give you the wedding you always imagined.

•

You can renew on a tenth, fifteenth, or twentieth an-niversary, but you can renew any other time as well.

•

By the time you have been married a number of years, you have survived a great deal as a couple and have created hundreds of memories. You can personally design your ceremony to reflect your own history, especially if you write your own vows.

•

Or you can be more traditional and either recite the same words that brought you together at your wedding or use the same officiant you had at your wedding.

•

Consider planning a surprise renewal for your spouse—use a milestone anniversary celebration as a chance to celebrate your marriage all over again.

•

Vow Renewal Benefits

♥   ♥   ♥   ♥   ♥

There are no hard-and-fast rules for a vow renewal ceremony. Feel free to be creative.

You don't need a legal officiant and need not comply with the legal requirements of a wedding. How freeing!

It is nice to be able to write your own vows without having any time limitations or restrictions imposed by the officiant.

You can even try to have your original wedding party members come to the wedding and serve as your attendants again.

Where to Renew Your Vows

♥   ♥   ♥   ♥   ♥

You can renew almost anywhere, in any country, at any location—even at locations where it would be difficult to get married.

♥

You can return to your exact wedding location and re-create your wedding.

♥

An exotic setting for the wedding, such as barefoot on a romantic beach at sunset or atop a mountain on horseback, will give your guests another reason to attend.

♥

Or, why not renew your vows at home? This location may truly be the most special place to renew your vows, since it is where you have built your life together.

♥

How to Renew Your Vows

♥   ♥   ♥   ♥   ♥

Renew your vows privately or publicly, whichever is your heart's desire. This is your chance to have the wedding you've always dreamed of, not just to replicate what you had years ago.

●

Have a theme vow renewal ceremony. (See the theme wedding ideas in chapter 8.)

●

Instead of traditional bridesmaids and groomsmen, ask important friends or relatives who are couples to be in your wedding party. Choose close friends who have weathered the years with you, as well as newer friends you have acquired during your years as a couple. In a traditional wedding the bridesmaids and groomsmen reflect the joining of two single people, while in a vow renewal celebration your attendants can be couples significant to your couplehood.

•

Some etiquette books say that when renewing your vows, you should not wear a veil or throw a bouquet, but if you wish you can wear a long wedding gown (perhaps your original one), and you can register again, too.

•

If you and your husband choose to walk down an aisle again, walk as a couple or as individuals coming together. You don't need to be "given away" again.

•

It is nice to exchange a token to represent your recommitment to each other, such as a necklace or even matching his-and-her watches to symbolize the timelessness of your love.

•

You don't have to exchange any material things, though. The words you share and the symbolic ceremony can be more than enough.

•

Invite guests to participate in your ceremony via readings, candle lightings, or singing.

•

If you have children, incorporate them into the ceremony, and remarry as a family unit.

•

Have your children write their own vows and exchange a gift or token with them.

•

Have a first dance to your wedding song.

•

Sharing Your Life with Your Guests

♥   ♥   ♥   ♥   ♥

Create a video or photo album of your years together, and share it with your guests. Be sure to include highlights or key events in your lives together.

Draw a timeline of life milestones and memorable events that you have shared together.

Display photos from your wedding and other memorabilia (your wedding favors, wedding certificate, scrapbook, family photos, and so on).

18

The Groom's Guide: What Else Do You Need to Do Besides Just Show Up?

Nowadays, grooms, your duty is not limited to just showing up at the ceremony. Brides and family members expect your participation and involvement in many aspects of the wedding planning process. For advice on proposing, consult the preface of this book, but be sure you read this chapter as well so that you are covered on all other counts.

Selecting Your Groomsmen

Choose your wedding party wisely, especially your best man. Not all of your fraternity brothers, childhood friends, or basketball buddies need to be included in the wedding party.

•

Think about who you can imagine yourself still being friends with twenty years down the road, and your choices should become clearer.

•

When planning male bonding events for the wedding weekend, stick with golf or spectator sports as opposed to risking injury in a group football or basketball game. A black eye or twisted ankle won't go over well on your wedding day.

•

Your best man should be the person you can most depend on in the whole world. His role is to walk the fine line between helping you celebrate your final days of bachelorhood and getting you to the ceremony in one piece and with no regrets.

•

Does the best man need to be a brother, brother-in-law, or future brother-in-law? If this man is the closest to you, then yes. If, however, your brother or brother-in-law is much younger and cannot handle the planning duties, or if he is very single and cannot grasp the importance of why you are getting married in the first place, then think about having your best friend do the honors.

•

If your bride has brothers that she wants you to include in your wedding party, consider doing so.

•

If you have already invited enough guys to be in your party, offer your bride's male friends the honor of being ushers (they seat guests but do not stand up at the wedding) or doing a reading. Readings can range from a personal poem selected by the bride and groom to a biblical passage pertinent to the ceremony. Or, readings can be poetic, meaningful reflections written by the designated reader to the bride and groom.

•

If you have a sister whom you'd like to see included in your bride's wedding party, it is only fair to offer to ask her brother to be in yours. Approach these family issues with sensitivity and open communication. Feelings can get hurt.

•

Guys are much more flexible and accommodating when it comes to sensitive issues regarding the wedding party. Plus, they can always be assigned the roles of ushers, program distributors, ketubah signers, chuppah holders, and even readers in your ceremony. Don't sweat it.

•

Provide your best man with a detailed schedule of the wedding events and a timetable of where and when things will occur. He should keep this handy as his guide throughout the events. (If you use a wedding coordinator, he or she can help you put this list together.)

•

On the wedding day, give your best man the rings, the officiant fee, a detailed schedule of the day, and all other pertinent items (breath mints, lip balm, wallet) to hold onto for you. He'll be your right-hand man.

•

The Bachelor Party

♥   ♥   ♥   ♥   ♥

Reassure your fiancée before the bachelor party, and discuss your expectations up front so there are no surprises.

Tell her that you love her before you leave for the evening.

Conduct yourself like a gentleman while remaining one of the guys. Remember, bachelor parties are more for the single guys of the bunch than for those who are married or engaged.

Talk to your best man or bachelor party planners about what you are comfortable with and what will not work for you. This is no time to be pressured into being one of the guys if it means your future marriage will be jeopardized.

Designate someone to be totally responsible for you in case things get a little crazy.

Be sure you call your fiancée before you get too inebriated to tell her that you love her.

Taking Care of Your Fiancée and Bride

♥   ♥   ♥   ♥   ♥

Remember who is the most important person in the wedding process: your bride. She is the reason this is all happening.

♥

Remind yourself why you chose each other, and be there for her every step of the way through this exciting and stressful process.

♥

Even if you are not planning to be involved in the day-to-day wedding planning aspects, at least choose a few specific areas to give your input. For example, most grooms have strong opinions about the music, food, and limousine or send-off transportation.

♥

Listen and communicate—a lot.

♥

Get away together for a date night or an engagement weekend. Pamper and indulge each other.

♥

If you are negotiating a prenuptial agreement, remember that heightened feelings may emerge. Keep your sense of humor, and keep the lines of communication wide open. Don't let this legal formality spoil your happiness (and if it seems like it is doing so, consider eliminating this step altogether).

♥

Show up at the end of a bridal shower to help her open gifts.

♥

To earn a gold star, bring flowers to your fiancée at the shower.

♥

To earn platinum-level stars, bring flowers for your mother and future mother-in-law at the shower.

♥

Buy her a wedding gift. Whether it be extravagant diamond earrings, a new outfit for the honeymoon, or a beautiful bouquet of flowers with a card sent to her dressing room on the wedding day, let her know you haven't forgotten her and want to present her with a symbol of your love.

♥

Have your wedding bands engraved with a meaningful message. The date and your names are fine, but you may want to surprise her with a short phrase, poem, or special term of endearment that only you two know.

♥

Proofread the engraving when you pick up the rings. Mistakes have been known to happen!

♥

Have a special handkerchief monogrammed with both of your married initials on it to hand her during the ceremony (or to use yourself!) if she starts to cry.

♥

Take care of your bride and compliment her often.

♥

Be supportive and involved (if she wants you to be) in the registering process.

♥

Other Groom Duties

♥   ♥   ♥   ♥   ♥

See if any of your local guy friends are willing to host out-of-town male guests. This can save money and hassles for some of your friends and family who are traveling great distances.

•

Most guys don't mind sleeping on floors or couches since the price is right!

•

Check into the policy on premarital blood testing in your state (or the state in which you are getting married). Some states require this in order to get married, so plan ahead.

•

Traditionally, you (or your side of the family) are responsible for paying for the wedding rings, rehearsal dinner, honeymoon, marriage license and officiant fees, boutonnieres for the groomsmen and other male honorees and family members, and sometimes even the cost of hotel accommodations for family and attendants.

•

Be the liaison between your bride and your parents. Don't put your bride in the middle of things and create bad feelings. You are responsible for your family, and she is responsible for hers.

•

Consider buying a tuxedo if you do not own one already. Chances are this is the time to invest so that you will look terrific on the big day, and so that you will have formal attire to wear to future black-tie events. Your investment will pay off quickly.

•

Arrange for the two of you to take dance lessons so you can learn some moves together and practice dancing to your wedding song. She'll love the gesture!

•

Plan an awesome honeymoon! (See chapter 19.)

•

Don't surprise her with your honeymoon destination unless you are certain she'll be thrilled. It is not worth the possibility of disappointment. This trip is for both of you.

•

19 ♥♥♥

Honeymoons

Grooms, fess up: Isn't the honeymoon the wedding-related event you're most looking forward to? To get away, relax, indulge, and celebrate your love as husband and wife? Read on for dozens of ideas that will inspire you so you'll be able to enjoy every minute of this special vacation.

Tips on How to Plan

♥   ♥   ♥   ♥   ♥

Consider how each of you handles long flights and how much travel time you are willing to dedicate to reaching your honeymoon destination. For example, if you are focusing on a tropical locale and your wedding is on the West Coast, Hawaii might be a better pick than the Caribbean.

•

If you would like to use a travel agent, find one whom you can trust or who has been recommended by other honeymooners.

•

Go to your local bookstore or the Internet and read, read, read.

•

If you cannot get enough time off for your honeymoon due to busy work or school schedules, consider a short weekend getaway following your wedding—then plan a bigger trip for later.

•

When you have narrowed down your choices of hotels or regions, compare what travel critics from books and magazines have to say about specific properties.

•

Don't rely solely on glossy hotel brochures to give you all of the information you need. Remember that they are marketing pieces, and do your homework.

•

Remind your travel agent to book your tickets and hotel with "honeymooners" attached to the reservations. Or do so yourself if you make your reservations directly.

•

Take your agent's emergency contact number with you on your honeymoon, just in case any complications arise.

•

At check-in, remind the hotel attendant that you are on your honeymoon. You may get a complimentary bottle of champagne or be upgraded to an especially private corner room or suite.

•

If you plan to go to two different resorts and one is significantly more luxurious than the other, go to the fancier one on your second destination. Save the best for last!

•

Where to Honeymoon

♥   ♥   ♥   ♥   ♥

Consider a "couples-only" resort where everyone there will be in love and showing it! Plus, most activities at those types of resorts revolve around couples, romance, and love.

Check to see if your honeymoon resort allows young children. Many family-oriented properties may disappoint you if you are trying to spend a secluded, romantic vacation together.

If appropriate, plan what one travel expert calls a "hybrid honeymoon": a vacation where you make both of your dream honeymoons come true. For example, if your bride wants a quiet, relaxing, lazy vacation and you prefer action-filled sightseeing adventures, find a place that can accommodate both of your visions, or plan a two-part honeymoon.

If you are having a destination wedding, you'll already be at your honeymoon spot after the event. Be sure to visit a hotel other than the one in which you were married—for variety, and so you'll feel as though there is a distinction between your wedding site and your honeymoon locale.

Hawaii is a super destination if you want to feel exotic yet remain in the United States. The Hawaiians *love* honeymooners and will demonstrate their aloha spirit time and again.

Europe is classy and offers total variety, since you can travel by rail from country to country depending on your preferences in food, language, scenery, and atmosphere.

South America and Mexico are also popular honeymoon destinations, especially when the U.S. dollar is strong.

Take the Honeymoon Survey below to help narrow your focus.

The Honeymoon Survey

Ask yourself some of the questions below to help decide where you want to go on your honeymoon.

Do you like lots of other people around or do you prefer your privacy?

♥

Do you like adventure and the outdoors or prefer a quiet escape?

♥

Do you have different interests and vacation goals?

♥

Do you want to plan your trip together?

♥

Do you want to use a travel agent?

♥

Off the Beaten Path . . .

♥   ♥   ♥   ♥   ♥

Head to the Poconos for an inexpensive and cheesy but also romantic and fun honeymoon. Many hotels offer heart-shaped bathtubs, private swimming pools, and fireplaces in the rooms.

•

Las Vegas is fun for honeymooners who want an active night life, great spa amenities, fabulous shows, and romantic honeymoon suites.

•

For total privacy, how about renting a houseboat or sailboat? Call your local visitors bureau and ask for the names of marinas and agencies that handle such boat rentals. Make sure your bride is not prone to seasickness, though!

•

Borrow or rent an RV and drive around the country. Maybe you have generous relatives or friends who will let you convert their RV into your own honeymoon love nest. Chill champagne in the refrigerator daily and enjoy!

•

If you get married in the United States, staying domestic and driving instead of flying is often worth it. How about combining sightseeing major landmarks and hitting the most romantic bed & breakfasts along the way?

•

Rent a private cabin in the woods or go camping to get away from it all.

•

Budget Honeymoons

♥   ♥   ♥   ♥   ♥

Go to an all-inclusive resort where you pay one flat fee up front, so there will be no surprises or shocks at the checkout counter. Most all-inclusives offer accommodations, meals, activities, drinks, and even honeymoon goodies for one fixed price.

Check into the major discount travel Internet sites for great air and hotel package deals.

If your wedding date permits or if you choose to postpone your honeymoon until a few months after the wedding, plan to travel during your destination's "off season" or "low season" for cheaper rates. Seasonal discounts are not offered everywhere and will differ by destination, so consult your hotel and plan your honeymoon travel accordingly.

If you are traveling by air, fly on off-peak days of the week. Sunday through Wednesday are the cheapest days to fly between cities for both departure and arrival.

Use frequent-flyer miles for your honeymoon. They are free and offer great flexibility (except for high-season blackout dates that may apply).

Whenever you book a hotel (or car rental), ask for all possible discounts. For example, check to see if they take the Entertainment card; have any promotions related to Diners Club, Visa, or other credit cards; offer any frequent-flyer-mile deals; or offer student, AAA, military, or government discounts or reduced honeymoon rates.

Read the fine print when booking any hotel's honeymoon package. Often the added perks, such as airport transfers, champagne, and hotel robes, wind up costing more than if you just booked directly with the hotel and paid separately for those extras.

Honeymoon Romance

♥   ♥   ♥   ♥   ♥

Be sure to pack some romantic items to have on hand. Scented candles, bubble bath, oils, chocolates, body paint, an instant camera, a book of love poems or romantic stories, a blank journal to write your romantic stories in together, lingerie, romantic CDs, feathers, and soft silky robes are some fun ideas.

♥

Pack music and mini-speakers for your portable CD player so you can enjoy your own romantic music in your hotel room.

♥

If your room will have a VCR, bring a "how-to" massage or other sensual video and practice with your partner.

♥

If you arrive at your hotel and find that your room does not meet your expectations, speak up immediately. Where you sleep (and play!) makes a lot of difference in the mood and tone of your honeymoon.

♥

Decorate your room to enhance the romantic mood. For example, put some scented oil on the light bulbs as soon as you check in. When the lights heat up, the fragrance may inspire romance.

♥

Book a special couple's massage or other romantic spa treatment you can do together if your resort offers it. Two masseuses or masseurs can even come to your room with soft music, candles, and scented oils and give you massages simultaneously.

♥

Spray your favorite special perfume or cologne on your sheets and pillows.

♥

Take a bubble bath.

♥

Light scented candles.

♥

Order room service, a fruit basket, or champagne and strawberries, and feed each other.

Final Nuts and Bolts

♥   ♥   ♥   ♥   ♥

Get traveler's checks for your trip. Have them in both your name and her maiden name so either of you can cash them.

•

Book your bride's tickets in her maiden name or, if you must use her married name, take a copy of your marriage certificate with you on your trip for identification purposes.

•

Make photocopies of your tickets, passports, traveler's check receipts, and any emergency phone numbers or other information you may need. Take these with you on your trip, and keep them in a separate place from the originals.

•

Don't write thank you notes on your honeymoon. This is the time to focus on the two of you and not do "homework."

•

Honeymoon disasters have been known to happen. If you experience one, just be sure to keep your sense of humor. They make for great stories afterward.

•

Grooms beware: Your wedding band may feel strange at first if you are not accustomed to wearing jewelry. Keep it on your finger at all times and be sure it is tight enough. One groom lost his while snorkeling and another lost his on the beach. Don't fiddle with it!

•

Keep a honeymoon journal together where you two can record your memories and save fun, small items such as ticket stubs from shows you watched or sightseeing you may have participated in, restaurant matchbooks, or other small souvenirs.

•

Be sure to pack a deck of cards, some good books, and Scrabble or any other games that you two will enjoy playing on your honeymoon. Things will be hectic and busy when you return to the real world, so enjoy this opportunity to drop out and play together.

•

20 ♥♥♥

Handling PWS, Part 2: Post-Wedding Syndrome

The honeymoon is over, the wedding but a memory. Now what? While you don't have to come down from cloud nine entirely, there are some tasks and details that you have to attend to: gift returns, thank you notes and name change issues. Welcome to the world of Mr. and Mrs.

Gift Returns

♥   ♥   ♥   ♥   ♥

Any duplicate items you receive should be returned for a full refund or store credit immediately.

•

If you can get cash back for a gift, choose that option. Be sure to put the money into a bank account specifically designated for items you'll need for your new life as husband and wife (unless, of course, you've both agreed to spend the money on tickets to an event or dinner out).

•

Check the store's policy on spending unused credit. Some allow you only one year to spend it.

•

If your gift comes from a small boutique or non–chain store, in lieu of store credit, try to pick out an alternative gift in exchange. Smaller stores may not stay in business forever, so it's better to spend your credit on a gift now than to lose the credit later.

•

If your china, crystal, or silver registries have been completed, consider getting a few additional place settings to allow for future breakage, loss, or damage. For example, if you registered for twelve place settings of china, you may want to purchase two extra sets, since patterns can be discontinued and dishes may break through the years. You'll keep yourself covered for a while by having some extra on reserve.

•

Just because you registered for something months ago and received it as a wedding gift does not mean that you'll necessarily like it today. Tastes and needs change. If you have doubts about something, by all means, return it and get something you really want.

•

Note that some gifts are not returnable. Artwork, special-order items, and personalized pieces are yours to keep.

•

If a gift is not your taste but the giver is special to you, tuck it away; if that guest ever comes to your home and expects to see it, pull it out of your closet to display.

•

Thank You Notes

♥　　♥　　♥　　♥　　♥

Hand-write thank you notes. Computer printing, e-mailing, or calling will not suffice.

Have stationery printed with your new married names or, at a minimum, your and your husband's first names. This is a very classy touch and your first opportunity to use your names together.

Try to hand-address your envelopes rather than use computer labels. It's perfectly okay to order envelopes with preprinted return addresses, though, and you'll save the time that you would have spent applying return address labels or writing the return addresses by hand.

Have a three-ring binder, index card, or computerized system in place where you keep a master list of each guest's name, the gift you received from him or her, the date of receipt, and the date you wrote the thank you note for the gift.

Your gift record organizer will become an invaluable reference for your future gift giving, as well as a useful memory aid to help you personally acknowledge the gifts of guests you see in person after the wedding.

※

Don't wait until after the wedding to write all the thank you notes. For gifts that arrive prior to the wedding, try to write notes before the big day.

※

Pace yourself when writing notes. Set a goal of ten notes per day or week depending on what you can handle, in order to preserve your sanity and keep the messages in your notes fresh. Don't feel that you have to get through all of them in a few sittings.

※

Keep in mind that modern brides aren't solely responsible for writing the thank you notes. Grooms should do their share, too.

※

At a minimum, if you write the majority of the thank you notes, assign your groom the tasks of licking and stamping envelopes, helping you come up with catchy thank you phrases, and mailing them (if you fully trust that he will!).

※

If there are certain guests that only one of you knows well (for instance, one of your bosses, a college roommate, or a childhood friend), that person should write the note.

※

For gifts that are solely monetary, it is nice to include in your thank you note what you plan to do with the money. For example, if you are putting it toward something big or using it to save for the future, indicate that in your note.

If a gift does not have a card attached, immediately contact the store where it was purchased (if that information is available). They may have a record of the purchaser. If not, after you have recorded all of your other gifts and noted who gave them to you, see if you can figure out by process of elimination who gave you the mystery gift.

If you receive a gift and you are not certain of its use or even what it is, contact the store where it was purchased (if that is evident) to see if they can assist you.

If you aren't able to determine what some gifts are, in your thank you notes, just thank the givers for their generous gifts, and use the remaining space to discuss the givers' role in your wedding celebration—or, if they did not attend, cite some wedding highlights.

Etiquette states that guests have up to one year from the wedding date to purchase your gift. So don't be surprised if gifts dribble in for months after your wedding.

Always write a thank you note for any gift received.

Thank You Gifts

♥   ♥   ♥   ♥   ♥

Give gifts to your parents to thank them for their contributions to your wedding—whether fiscally, emotionally, or just generally.

♥

Give a token of thanks as well as a nice note to anyone who organized a brunch, shower, bachelor or bachelorette party, or rehearsal dinner.

♥

If the priest, caterer, florist, photographer, or musicians clearly exceeded your expectations or went beyond the call of duty at your wedding, consider sending them a token of thanks as well as a personal thank you note citing specific examples of how they assisted you.

♥

Your hired help will be pleased to use your notes of thanks as references for future brides and grooms, so be sure to give credit where it is due.

♥

Appropriate gifts, depending on what you want to spend, include a nice bottle of wine or champagne, a fruit basket, a ceramic or glass memento, a paperweight or piece of glass with your wedding date engraved or etched on it, a gift certificate, or flowers.

♥

Inquire at bridal shops or wedding magazines about companies that specialize in invitation preservation. This is a wonderful souvenir that you two can give to each other or to your parents as a thank you gift.

♥

If You Change Your Name

♥   ♥   ♥   ♥   ♥

Send in all the necessary documents as soon as possible.

•

Make many photocopies of your marriage license so you can fax or mail your name change to the appropriate parties.

•

Notify all your credit card companies, your bank, the Social Security Administration, your health insurance provider, your alma mater, your employer, and any other necessary parties.

•

Obtain an extra original, notarized copy of your marriage license. It is easier to order an extra one now, when your original is being processed, than to reorder one later.

•

If you have children whose names will change as a result of your marriage, deal with this changeover promptly.

•

If you are opening or have opened a joint bank account with your husband, be sure the bank has your married names in its system so both of you will be able to access funds.

•

For fun, order new stationery with your married names on it and have things monogrammed such as sheets, towels, and robes to celebrate your new status as husband and wife.

•

Emotional Survival

♥   ♥   ♥   ♥   ♥

Some couples ease smoothly into married life, while others struggle with new issues of shared expenditures, living arrangements, and geographic issues. Remind yourselves why you got married in the first place.

Remember to laugh a lot.

Communicate often.

Court each other again and again.

Say "I love you" or demonstrate your love daily.

Cherish each other.

Keep your sense of humor.

Don't go to bed angry.

Try new things together.

Savor the passing moments.

Watch your wedding video whenever you need a glowing reminder of why you two got married in the first place.

You have survived one of the toughest, most emotional highs (or lows) of your relationship: getting married. Now enjoy building the future that lies ahead as husband and wife.

Conclusion

I hope that you have gleaned some ideas from the hundreds offered here. Just know that planning a wedding from beginning to end can be an overwhelming and stressful process, but with some clever ideas and your sense of humor, you can have fun and enjoy this romantic, exciting, and unforgettable experience. Wishing you a wonderful beginning together and a happily ever after.

Send Me Your Ideas

If the ideas in this book have inspired you or if you or someone you know has clever wedding ideas to share, I want to know about them.

Please e-mail your submissions to:

MarryMe123@aol.com
or fax a copy of your ideas in writing to:
(949) 644-4135

Index

About the Author

Cynthia C. Muchnick was born and raised in Marin County, California. She pursued her undergraduate degree in Art History and Political Science at Stanford University where she met her husband, Adam Muchnick. After completing college, Cindy moved to Chicago where she began her career in college admissions at the University of Chicago. Cindy and her husband relocated to Florida where she earned her masters degree

Photo by Eliot Holtzman

in Liberal Studies, taught tenth grade history, and wrote her first book, *Will You Marry Me?* After the overwhelming success of her first book, Cindy wrote a follow-up book, *101 Ways to Pop the Question*.

Cindy is proud to be dubbed an Engagement Expert and Coach. She has appeared on dozens of talk shows and news programs including *Leeza, Sally Jesse Raphael, Donny & Marie, Fox News, Good Day LA, Good Day New York*, and many others. Cindy also worked as a columnist and spokesperson for *Honeymoon Magazine* and freelanced for *Coast Magazine*. Her educational publication, *The Best College Admission Essays*, is a how-to book for high school students going through the college essay writing process.

Still incurable romantics, Cindy and Adam are living happily ever after with their two sons in Southern California. For an insider's advice on popping the question, to book the author as a motivational speaker, or to order signed copies of her books, e-mail Cindy at MarryMe123@aol.com.